THE
Perfectly Trained

Rebecca K. O'Connor

The Perfectly Trained Parrot

Editor: Tom Mazorlig
Indexer: Dianne L. Schneider
Designer: Mary Ann Kahn

TFH Publications®
President/CEO: Glen S. Axelrod
Executive Vice President: Mark E. Johnson
Editor-in-Chief: Albert Connelly, Jr.
Production Manager: Kathy Bontz

TFH Publications, Inc.®
One TFH Plaza
Third and Union Avenues
Neptune City, NJ 07753

Printed and bound in China
14 15 16 17 18   1 3 5 7 9 8 6 4 2

Library of Congress Cataloging-in-Publication Data
O'Connor, Rebecca.
  The perfectly trained parrot / Rebecca K. O'Connor.
    pages cm
  Includes index.
  ISBN 978-0-7938-0720-8 (alk. paper)
  1. Parrots--Training. I. Title.
  SF473.P3O264 2013
  636.6'865--dc23
                          2012041532

This book has been published with the intent to provide accurate and authoritative information in regard to the subject matter within. While every reasonable precaution has been taken in preparation of this book, the author and publisher expressly disclaim responsibility for any errors, omissions, or adverse effects arising from the use or application of the information contained herein. The techniques and suggestions are used at the reader's discretion and are not to be considered a substitute for veterinary care. If you suspect a medical problem consult your veterinarian.

The Leader In Responsible Animal Care for Over 50 Years!®
www.tfh.com

Table of Contents

Introduction

This book could change your life. I don't just mean that it could make living with your parrot more fun and enjoyable, although I certainly hope it does that. Hopefully, that is why you are reading! What I mean by changing your life is that understanding how to communicate with and train wild animals can shift the way you see the world. It can also help you change the world—or at least your area of it. This may seem like a bold statement for beginning a little parrot training book, but I do believe the years I have spent trying to understand and interact with the animals in my life have taught me how to shape my surroundings into a positive, happy place.

When I give lectures I joke constantly about training ex-boyfriends and using positive reinforcement on the people in my life. The audience laughs, I laugh, and we all pretend that I'm kidding—but I'm not. For example, just saying "thank you" when a person does something you like is a great start to shaping behavior with positive reinforcement. The way the people in your life act to get your

Learning about and applying positive reinforcement will make the relationship with your parrot more harmonious.

attention can often be directly correlated to how you react or don't react to their methods (reinforcement, in trainer language—there's a lot more on this topic later). If your best friend loves hour-long conversations on the phone and the only way she can get you to stay on the phone is to call with a crisis, guess what? When you stay on the phone, you are reinforcing her. You better enjoy listening to her latest breakdown, because she is going to call with them, often.

Applied behavior analysis is an ethical way to shape behavior in most situations.

Your actions really do speak louder than your words. More importantly, your actions shape how everyone interacts with you. Behaviors that work—meaning produce the desired result—in an individual's environment are repeated. This is the basis of behavioral learning theory. ("Theory" meaning an established explanation of phenomena used in science, rather than an unproven guess, which has become the more common usage.) So if you allow an individual's behaviors to work when you don't like what they are doing—in other words, the person gets what they want through their undesirable behavior—you may be creating an unhappy living situation. Shaping behavior and understanding what triggers it and reinforces it is the core of the psychology of human behavior analysis, and a basic understanding of this is actually critical to training your parrot as well.

If you understand the underlying communication of training, you can have a perfect parrot. Yes, I said, "perfect". I was given a bit of grief over my last parrot book's having the words "perfect parrot" in the title. There were those who felt I was encouraging unrealistic expectations of parrots. So let me clarify. The English language is alive, and the definitions of words evolve. We rarely use the word "perfect" with its original intent of being flawless, as a diamond can be. So few things in this world are that kind of perfect, yet we use the word all the time. I've gone out on dates with a few perfect gentlemen, but they were far from flawless. Thank goodness for that too, because flawless is boring. We all have quirks and annoying behaviors. The trick to living happily with any human or animal is to make concessions for the habits that do not bother us all that much and clearly communicate how to live happily together. A perfect parrot is one that gives you great joy, is healthy and well-adjusted, and has minor and livable-with bad habits. A perfect parrot has everything to do with your ideal standard. What you need to do is decide what that standard is and make it fun to live up to it. Trust me. Your parrot has his own ideal standards of how you should behave as well. The two of you can have this conversation with applied behavior analysis.

Applied behavior analysis is a straightforward and ethical way to shape behavior in most, if not all, situations. Whether it is used in special education with children, managing zoo animals, or communicating with the parrot in your living room, it is applicable, replicable, and sensible. In this book it will be the basis for training and problem solving. Once you start practicing on your parrot(s), though, you may find that you get better at expressing what you mean to the whole world. You may find that you are clearer and more consistent and that everyone else seems to be as well. Life gets less stressful. Days are more enjoyable. Relationships are full of joy. It sounds like a miracle, but it's nothing more than clarity and better communication.

I can hear you now as I type this, "That's great, Rebecca, but all I want is for my parrot to wave on cue." I understand, and we will get right at that. All the same, if you find that you really enjoy training, become excellent at it, and suddenly life gets even better, don't say I didn't warn you!

Happy Training!
Rebecca K. O'Connor

1

Where Do I Begin?

I f you have never trained a pet, the idea of teaching your parrot to do anything might be a little daunting to you. Birds can be particularly challenging because we do not know how to read their body language or understand how to respond to it. Perhaps you already have had some moments with your bird where you just could not fathom why he bit you or acted the way he did. It can take some practice learning what a parrot is saying with his body language and knowing how best to react to what he is trying to tell you. In fact, when we are first working with parrots we often guess why our parrots do the things they do, assuming that their motivations would be similar to our own. So where do you begin when you decide you want to know how to train your bird?

Training the Animals in our World

Imagine that your parrot is an alien dropped into your home from another world.

Things to Learn About Your Parrot

If you are about to get a parrot or have not learned a whole lot about the one you have, here are three things to look into:

- Where does this species live in the wild?
- Knowing whether your bird comes from the rainforest or the savannah can tell you a lot about his natural behavior and the activities he will enjoy and engage in quickly. A parrot that spends a lot of time on the ground in the wild may likely be more comfortable on the floor than on a perch, for example.
- When does and where does this parrot breed in the wild?
- What time of the year would your parrot breed in the wild? Aggression and nesting behavior can be linked to a change in hormones. And if your parrot is a hollow nester, you may want to avoid the brooding behavior that it encouraged by going into dark cavities.
- What other natural behaviors can you find out about?
- Does your parrot species wrestle with its buddies and roll around on the ground in the wild? You will probably have a lot of luck teaching your parrot to lie on his back and play dead. Find out what you can about wild behavior and come up with new training tricks that mimic wild behaviors.

Actually, this is pretty close to the truth. Overall they have strange expressions that do not make sense at first, mostly based in the rise and fall of feathers. Parrots don't have lips and cannot smile. They communicate in clicks and beeps. Their strange little pupils expand and contract with their thoughts. Even their locomotion is different from ours. It is hard to even imagine what it would feel like to travel through the world on wings, but they do it and make it look easy. You may as well have E.T. in

Having a pet parrot is a little like living with an extraterrestrial—parrots' motivations, behavior, and communication are alien to you.

your living room. (If you haven't seen the movie *E.T.: the Extraterrestrial*, you should definitely rent it.)

Yet despite the fact we must seem just as alien to them, we assume parrots understand our words, motions, and sometimes even our thoughts. So where would you start if you found yourself having to share your home with an alien you wanted to communicate with, have fun with, and teach how best to live with you? If it were E.T. you would coax it into interacting with you with candy, train it how to integrate into your home without making too much trouble, teach it to talk, learn everything you could about the species, and then work on some awesome tricks together. (Who wouldn't want to ride a flying bicycle?) You should skip the candy, but working with a parrot is not all that different from working out how to live with E.T.

Knowing about your bird's natural history is crucial to understanding his behavior.

Who Are You?

The best place to start is by learning everything you can about the parrot in your life. This means learning about both the history of your individual parrot and your parrot's species (and sometimes the subspecies) and how that species lives in nature.

Your Bird's Biography

Your parrot's past is nice to know if you have a bird that has been adopted from a rescue or previous owner (a rehomed parrot), but don't get hung up on it. People have a habit of assuming the worst about an animal's past and then believing that this past is a hurdle that must be jumped over before your new friend will be "whole" again. The vast majority of the time, this is simply not true. Parrots are resilient, brilliant, engaging birds that quickly adjust to a new home, especially if it is a positive and enriching environment. Except in the most extreme cases, you have a brand new start with your parrot, and the way he behaves will have to do with how you interact with him. He may have a few quirks and fears, but don't we all?

Don't make the assumption that your parrot has come to you "broken," but if you can, find out what his past experiences were. If your parrot has never stepped up for someone before, you will have some work to do training him. If you are told that his owner always picked him up by having him step onto a stick, you may need to take some time training him to step up onto hands. If he has always been fed only sunflower seeds and peanuts, you may need to train him to explore new foods and develop new tastes. Information such as this is helpful, but it certainly isn't mandatory. You don't have to have any information about his past to work with him. If you begin training as if everything is new and anything is possible, you will surely have success. You do, however, need to know about your parrot's natural history.

Your Bird's Natural History

Even if you are bringing home a young parrot that has never lived in another home, the more you know about the species you are living with the better. A parrot's behaviors will have a great deal to do with what members of its species naturally do in the wild. Is your parrot a ground feeder? A cavity nester? What is its natural diet? Find out everything you can about your bird.

What's the Difference?

Applied behavior analysis, operant conditioning, behavior modification, and behavior therapy are all basically the same thing, referring to the same strategies of training. They are not interchangeable terms, but so similar in nature that they are all often used to describe the same techniques. However, applied behavior analysis is a comprehensive and rigorous approach to shaping and changing behavior that in its true definition involves systematic and defined methodology. A full understanding of the application of behavior analysis is a wonderful way to problem-solve difficult behavior issues.

The Internet can be a great resource, but be careful about where your information originates. The law of the Internet seems to be that the more it is repeated, the more likely it is to be believed. Unfortunately, it also seems that the more it is repeated the more likely it is to be misinformation. Look for your information in scientific papers, nationally respected magazines, and from well-known scientists, not from bulletin boards and Facebook. Once you know all you can about your parrot, it's time to bring him home and start training.

Who's Training Who?

Don't think you are ready to train? The good news is that the basics and practice are all you need. In fact, you are probably already training your parrot if you have one in your home. If there are behaviors that your parrot repeats, you have likely trained them for better or for worse. The trick is to be mindful and to begin training only the things you appreciate and enjoy. Polish your training skills to

What if My Parrot Isn't Trainable?

Every bird is an individual, just as every parrot owner is too. People frequently ask me what the hardest species of bird to train is and my answer is always that they are all just different. Every bird has a different personality, even within a species. Some parrots, like many cockatoos, tend to not have much food motivation. Some parrots, like most lories and lorikeets, have high energy. There are also parrots that are standoffish. Many African greys I have met are very standoffish, but I have met a couple of greys that are as social as a parrot can be.

A parrot's personality can make him more difficult to train or less difficult, depending on the trainer and what the trainer is hoping to teach. And just like all other animals (including people), there are parrots who have a real knack and desire for learning while many others do not. If you have multiple parrots you may find that one parrot is easier to train than the others. Or perhaps one is great at mimicking new sounds and one is wonderful at physical behaviors. No parrot is entirely untrainable, not even yours. You just need to take the time, have the patience, and focus on your parrot's positive attributes.

Training is about having a conversation with your parrot. In each interaction, be mindful of what you are saying to him.

the point of feeling comfortable training new behaviors and having fun with your parrot while doing it.

Perhaps the most important thing to understand about training is that it is primarily about having a conversation with your parrot. Training is not about "making" an animal do anything. It is also not about bribing, coercing, or starving. Training is about building a two-way street where both of you are conversing about what the other wants and coming to an agreement.

For example, when your bird receives positive attention from you, you are communicating you feel that whatever the parrot was doing at that moment deserves a reward. Perhaps your parrot called out, "Yoohoo!" and you wandered over to scratch him on the head. If your parrot liked getting attention and wants some more of it, he will do it again. You are giving your parrot a way to say "Hey, pay attention to me," which gets him the response he wants. You are saying to him, "Sure thing. I'll come visit with you. I like it when you call out 'yoohoo' instead of screaming." You are happy. The parrot is happy— and all of this was training. Unfortunately, sometimes we forget that this is training and have a communication breakdown.

Such is often the case with a parrot who screams. (By screaming, I mean calling out noisily, frequently, and repetitiously). A parrot who screams has been rewarded to do so. Often, screaming happens just with day-to-day actions and without your realizing that you trained it. Remember that training is conversation. Perhaps your parrot began with a yell or two to get

Falcons were among the first birds that people trained. This is the author with her falcon.

your attention and to ask you to come over and visit. If you walked over and calmly told your parrot to, "Please hush," he probably did for a minute. After all, he called for you and you came over to visit. To him, you had a very clear conversation and your end of it was, "just yell for me and I'll be right over." Maybe you get annoyed with being yelled at and stop coming right away. Over time it takes you five minutes or so of yelling before you finally can't take it and walk over to tell him a little less patiently to hush. Now you have clearly told him that the way to get your attention is to yell for at least five minutes. Guess what? You've trained your parrot to scream.

Parrots are intelligent and constantly interacting with their environment. The way they behave and what they learn to do has a lot to do with how you and the rest of the household respond to them. That is how it works in the wild. Parrots develop behaviors based on how their flock interacts with them and what happens in their environment. So parrots pay close attention to what your actions are saying.

Don't make the mistake of thinking your parrot knows automatically what you want or even cares about that. Maybe parrots do make guesses at what we are thinking, but if they do, I doubt they are any better at it than we are at guessing what a parrot is thinking. Most of the time we don't even guess right about what the people around us are thinking. So if you learn how to think like a trainer and make your actions very clear to your parrot, you are going to have a much happier household. If you don't work on training the parrot, the parrot is going to figure out how to train you instead.

The Beginnings of Animal Training

Animal training has been around for perhaps as long as people have interacted with animals. Although the psychology and techniques of training animals have evolved, especially in the last century, there is nothing new about humans wanting to teach animals to work with them. Humans may have begun training dogs as long as 15,000 years ago. Over time we have created breeds with specialties in following a scent, pointing or flushing quarry, and even hunting game. Training animals has been a keystone of civilization from its beginnings, but not just training domesticated animals.

Before there were firearms, falconers all over Europe and Asia worked with a variety of raptors to hunt with them. Unlike cats and dogs, bred for their desire to interact with us, raptors were not domesticated. Taken from the wild and painstakingly trained to take down winged and ground quarry, falcons and hawks were an effective means to bring meat to the banquet hall. Falconry too is not a new means of training and has been practiced for more than 3,000 years. Some of the first detailed books on animal training were written by falconers. Frederick II of Hohenstaufen wrote *The Art of Falconry*, a detailed treatise on training in the 1200s, and translations of it are still in print and read by falconers today.

People were also successfully training animals that you probably don't even consider as trainable. Cheetahs were trained to work with people and hunt gazelle in India and Afghanistan. Working with cheetahs was still in favor with Indian royalty in the early 1900's. Elephants have been trained to work with people for 4,000 years. Captured from the wild, the individuals that adjusted the best were trained and spent their lives often with one trainer. In modern times they have been primarily used for logging, but in ancient times rulers used elephants as an instrument of war. Famous leaders such as Hannibal had war elephants on the battlefield as part of their armies.

While people trained a wide variety of wild animals, parrots remained mostly ornaments. Parrot fanciers looked at parrots more as beautiful and unique additions to their homes rather than as working or even performing animals. Certainly as parrots became more common, species with a propensity to speak were encouraged to learn household words. There may have been a few people out there training their parrots to do interesting things, but for the most part parrots were not considered standard pets or working animals. This attitude prevailed until recent times as well.

When I was doing bird shows, it was not uncommon for people to refer to "animals and birds," as if birds were something entirely different. In fact, there were times when people spoke to me in awe that it was even possible to train a bird. Birds for the most part, in their opinion, were useless. Because I had worked with birds since I was a little girl, I found this to be absurd. Training birds was no harder than training any other animal once you could read them. The only difference between the people who thought birds were untrainable and me was that I had more practice.

Animal Training Today

The world of training animals has changed significantly, but many people still see birds—including parrots—as animals that are content to sit in a cage and while away their lives with a bowl of seed in front of them. This is tragic because the possibilities for interaction and fun with a parrot are limitless. Fortunately, modern psychology has given us insights into the way all living creatures react and adapt within their environments. It is possible to communicate and train anything with an agenda, as long as you can provide the proper reinforcement to make your point. I have seen goldfish trained to do agility courses in their aquariums. Surely training a parrot should be a piece of cake!

Superstition

From the early beginnings of training came a great deal of superstition and heavy-handed training. Without the scientific theories to explain why an animal responded in a certain

You can train for a wide range of behaviors using the concepts of operant conditioning and applied behavior analysis.

way, many experts created their own theories about how behavior worked. These systems of training often became lists of what a potential trainer should never do (Never let a parrot get above your head.) or what they should always do (Always ignore it when a parrot bites you.). The trainers did not really know how or why these rules worked. For example, their experience was that if they let a parrot get higher than them, they could not get the parrot down and sometimes got bitten. "This is just how parrots are!" a superstitious trainer might tell you. Therefore, you should never let this happen.

Superstition does not help you train, however. It merely gets in the way. If you understand applied behavior analysis you could break this behavior down and see that the parrot is actually being reinforced—he's getting what he wants. You just have to work on shaping the behavior to fix it. I let my parrots get above me all the time. They love the view, but they love the peanut they get when they come down as asked even better.

Using solely positive methods, the author has trained a wide variety of birds to perform.

Negative Training

Training in the past has frequently been based heavily on negative reinforcement and punishment. We will get into what these terms mean specifically later, but for now just think of the examples of a tiger trainer with the whip or a dog that gets his nose rubbed in the accident he had on the floor. You will see as we discuss training further that not all negative reinforcement or punishment is bad, it's simply not the most effective way to train most of the time. What it is, though, is fast and simple. It is easy to be impressed by someone who can grab an aggressive bird, force it into submission and then present the audience with a seemingly tamed and loving animal. There are psychological reasons why this works quickly and for a period of time, but it can have repercussions. And why use negative techniques when there are more effective methods for the long term? This is what animal trainers started asking themselves when B.F. Skinner introduced the world to operant conditioning.

Operant Conditioning

B.F. Skinner is known for his Project Pigeon. Funded by the military, he worked to train pigeons to guide bombs and torpedoes during World War II. Although the research and work was eventually dismissed as impractical, it wasn't without some small successes. Building on this research, Skinner defined operant conditioning and went on to lay the groundwork for behavior analysis.

While training rats and pigeons in the 1940s, Skinner opened up a new way to look at behavior, and his work had wide-ranging applications. Building on work done by Ivan Pavlov (Pavlov was the scientist who discovered that by pairing the ringing of a bell with the presentation of food, he could get dogs to salivate simply by ringing a bell.), Skinner studied the connection between stimuli and observable behavior. Skinner proved that behavior could be shaped if the operator was in control, voluntarily modifying the subject's behavior based on the consequence. For example, if given the choice to get corn for pecking a button or to do nothing and get nothing, a chicken will choose to peck the button. This is operant conditioning. Skinner also demonstrated that behavior could be shaped using operant conditioning and by breaking a given behavior into small steps and rewarding those steps. Skinner proved how important consequences are to creating behavior.

Animal Behavior Enterprises

Skinner's students Keller Breland and Marian Breland took these theories further to investigate how behavior analysis and operant conditioning could be applied to animal training outside the lab. They founded Animal Behavior Enterprises (ABE) in 1947, which was the first commercial business to take these techniques and apply them to real- world animals. To make a living they had to train more than just rats and pigeons, so the animals they trained were diverse. Mostly these animals were employed in the entertainment industry and as commercial ambassadors. The Brelands' clients were varied and included the military, theme parks, and even large companies like General Mills. When Keller Breland passed away, Marian kept the business going and eventually hired Bob Bailey, who was previously Director of Animal Training for the U.S. Navy. Over the life of the company, ABE trained over 15,000 animals and more than 150 species.

The impact of ABE on the animal training world was immense. Keller and Marian were the inventors of the clicker, which started its life as a little tin "cricket." They also coined the term "bridging stimulus." Using a clicker to mark a requested behavior before handing over a treat proved to be immensely effective and greatly reduced the amount of time it took to train a behavior. The duo hoped that clickers would take off with people training their pets at home in the 1940s and 1950s, but perhaps they were before their time.

The company contracted with many marine mammal and bird shows and was ultimately responsible for spreading the use of operant conditioning in training parrots during the 1950s and 1960s. Animal Behavior Enterprises shut down in 1990, but Bob Bailey still works in the field of animal training. His chicken camps,

Clever Hans

Clever Hans was a horse trained by a German mathematics teacher William von Osten, in the early 1900s. The horse was said to be able to do arithmetic, read, spell, and perform other tasks. By pawing at the ground with his hoof, the horse would answer yes, no, spell, or count. Von Osten gave no obvious clues, and it seemed that anyone who asked the horse a question could usually elicit a correct answer. However, careful examination by a board of experts revealed the horse relied on very subtle cues and stopped pawing based on the expression and stance of the questioner. Hans answered questions correctly only if the questioner knew the answer and Hans could see him. Just like Hans, your parrot will learn to read your body language and cues quickly. Be careful to be clear with your body language and to not fall under the spell of a "Clever Hans."

Small treats let your parrot get back to training quickly. This photo shows a good-sized treat for an African grey.

where he teaches aspiring animal trainers operant conditioning principles by training chickens, are still popular in Europe; animal trainers revere him.

Misunderstanding Skinner

Unfortunately, Skinner's techniques have often been poorly explained and therefore misunderstood. Some people interpret them to mean that an animal has no mind of its own but instead is just a stimulus-response machine. Believing that that is the basis of these techniques, they take offense at the implication that animals do not have feelings or thoughts of their own. This simply is not the point of operant conditioning. Animals are certainly thinking, feeling beings. In fact, in some cases their bond with us is part of the reinforcement and speeds training along. Instinct and natural behaviors play a role in behavior, and every facet of working with an animal does not boil down to simply "click and treat." Still, applied behavior analysis is the most effective means of training. These

Training through positive reinforcement will help you build a close relationship with your bird.

techniques are just making the communication clearer in a conversation we would be trying to have anyway.

Another issue that people sometimes have with these techniques is the belief that they are nothing more than manipulation. Even worse to people who feel this way is the idea that operant conditioning can be used to shape human behavior, which seems devious and even unconscionable to them. I once had a heated argument with my brother on a lovely beach in Mexico over the idea that I might write a book about using operant conditioning in your dating life. My brother was appalled that I would be so manipulative to a boyfriend, and no amount of tropical drinks or hours of beachfront view would change his mind. Still, his reaction was an emotional one rather than logical one. (Sorry, little brother!) Manipulation requires tactics such as trickery, bullying, and nagging. Good luck getting any of those techniques to work on a parrot. Operant conditioning using positive reinforcement hinges on appreciating and rewarding the good. I would much rather get a hug for picking up my laundry than be nagged for leaving it on the floor. Wouldn't you?

The Next Level
Today well-known animal trainers and behaviorists continue to teach and find new applications for operant conditioning and applied behavior analysis. Building

on the things we have learned from Skinner and the Brelands, trainers have discovered positive ways to train animals to do an incredible variety of things that improve their quality of life. Rather than capturing or sedating animals at zoos, trainers have used operant conditioning and positive reinforcement to teach them to present body parts for the veterinarian to inspect. There are even macaws that have been trained to sit still for annual vaccination injections in their breast muscles. It is becoming apparent that with time, patience, and positive reinforcement you can train animals in just about anything.

Building a Foundation

Perhaps now you are wondering why you were just given a summary of the entire history of animal training. Hopefully you found it interesting. An understanding of where these training techniques came from is important because they are proven techniques. There is nothing new about what I'm going to share with you. I'm just going to try to make it as simple and applicable as possible.

Even if you don't entirely understand or remember the terminology, you should be able to grasp the basics and have a lot of fun and success. And the great thing about training with a scientific basis is that if you get stuck or are ready to tackle more than is in this book there are tons of good reliable resources. These are all techniques that I have used training animals professionally as well as personally—I

Do Treats Have to be Healthy?

You should always be careful about your parrot's diet. Some parrot species are prone to obesity, and any parrot can become overweight. You should also never feed a parrot chocolate, caffeine, or anything that might be poisonous. The *occasional* bit of unhealthy food from the table is okay in moderation, however. I have used cookies, peanut butter pretzels, and even Cheetos for training. I prefer sunflower seeds, almonds, apples, and pine nuts, but every parrot has a different idea of the perfect treat. Also some foods are easier to dole out as a treat than others. Sticky, gooey treats can be problematic. Use your common sense, but reward with what works.

am certainly not the only one! There are online and in-person workshops, videos, and other trainers who use all these terms and techniques as well. In a book I don't have the luxury of rephrasing my explanation until it clicks with you as I would in a workshop. So if something in the book confuses you, you might find that one of these other resources uses scenarios or explanations that give you that "aha" moment that has eluded you. So let's get started!

What Do I Need to Start Training?

You do not need a whole lot of equipment to start training your parrot other than a handful of treats. As we get into specific behaviors that require props there will be some necessary items, but you do not need to buy anything to get started. If you prefer training with a clicker or would like to try training with a clicker, you can buy one of those. (There is a thorough explanation of clickers in the Event Markers section of Chapter 2.) Most chain pet stores carry them and they are not very expensive. A perch on a stand is helpful but not completely necessary to start. So don't fuss about all the goodies, just read through the techniques and terms carefully and get started. You'll need to return to them to remind

All you really need to start training is your parrot and a few treats.

yourself, but if they have trouble sticking in your head, don't worry. I have to remind myself sometimes, and I've been training for a long time. You don't have to be able to recite training terminology to understand it. What you need is reminders and practice—lots of practice.

Treats

The first thing you need to consider is what will be reinforcing to your parrot. We are going to train using strictly positive reinforcement, so you need to give some thought to what you can give your parrot that he will enjoy. For some parrots a scratch on the head or a cuddle is good reinforcement. However, kisses and cuddles are not the easiest way to train. Sometimes we misread our parrots and do not notice that they are tired of the training game and do not feel like being cuddled anymore. An unwanted cuddle can quickly turn into negative reinforcement and undermine a good training session.

Food is the easiest reinforcement because when your parrot is done with the treats and the training he will simply turn up his beak and stop taking food from you. This is clear and easy to understand. So training with treats is a good starting

place. Every parrot has different tastes, and you likely know your parrot's favorite treat. It doesn't hurt to experiment some. You may find an assortment of things your parrot loves. A great way to discover favorites is by mixing a bunch of different treats in your parrot's bowl when you give him the morning or evening meal. Whichever treat he chooses first will probably be the one that he likes best. Many parrots have favorites like peanuts, almonds, pine nuts, or even apples or pasta. Pay attention over time to which few treats he eats first and use those for training.

You do not have to starve your bird to train him. In fact, you do not need to cut back on his food at all. Give him all he wants to eat, but pull his favorite treats out of his diet and save these for training. If you want to make sure he has a little extra motivation, try training him right before you put a meal in his cage. Then give him a bowl full of food

One of the best training tools is a notebook. You can sketch out plans for training and take notes on the results.

when the training session is over. These treats will be all you need to get started training.

Set Yourself up to Succeed

While you don't need a lot of props to get started, there are few things you can do to help yourself succeed. Keep in mind that the key to training success is consistency. This sounds simple, but it is actually challenging for all us. We forget where we left off, decide to try different things midstream, or don't focus on rewarding at the right time. Simply put, we become poor communicators. We confuse our parrots. The only way to be consistent, especially if you are a new trainer, is to have a plan.

Start your training with a notebook and a pen. As you work your way through this book, jot down the key training concepts in the front of the notebook so that you can remind yourself before you start training sessions. Then for every behavior write out a plan. Sketch out what it is you want to train for and the steps involved. This will help you remind yourself not to skip steps, rush, or go too slow. This will make more sense as we begin to break down the process of training later in the book, but you may want to get your notebook ready now.

The most important purpose your notebook will serve is as a diary. When you are working with your bird, especially if things are going well, it seems as though there is no way you could forget what happened. Believe me, though, you will forget. Write down how long the session lasted, what time it was, what you used for treats, how motivated your parrot was, and what steps in the training you worked on. Make sure you note how and where in the training the session ended. This will help you pick up where you left off. And if you jot down as much as you can, you will start to notice patterns. For instance you may see in your notes that your parrot is losing interest more and more quickly each session. If you recognize this pattern you can fix it before your parrot refuses to play along at all. Maybe you just need to mix up the treats.

We kept notes for all the birds in the shows where I worked, and I have kept a notebook for every raptor I have trained in the last seventeen years. You never know when these notes might come in handy either. I found myself re-reading notes on a brown goshawk I trained in Australia ten years ago, a very similar bird to the Cooper's hawk I found myself working with this summer. I was surprised at how relevant my notes on her behavior were to the bird I was working with and how much this helped me. Keep a training journal. You won't regret it! So gather up your notebook and treats and let's look at the concepts you should understand before you begin training in your first behavior.

Stories of the Ruckus

The grandfather who raised me passed away when I was 24, and I fell silent for a week. I moped around my apartment ignoring parrots, leaving my red-tailed hawk in her mews, and mourned. My grandmother had also passed away three years earlier and I couldn't shake the thought that there was no one left who had witnessed my childhood. There was no one to tell tales of my hijinx, to remember what I had forgotten, and to argue about what I misremembered. They were gone, a childhood of shared stories gone with them.

I had lived with my grandparents from the time I was four until I went away to college. These were years full of birds, from the first fledgling found to the recalcitrant crows I bought from the local bird farm, to the Christmas cockatiel that became my first parrot. My grandfather encouraged my feather fancy from the very first day. In retrospect, I believe this gave him dual pleasure, that of my joy and of my grandmother's terror. She was petrified of the combination of confined spaces and free-flying birds. And my companions were often on the loose. I was a quiet and careful little girl, but the bird ruckus was allowed and I embraced it.

With both of my grandparents gone, I thought the ruckus was gone with them and the stories and memories should be allowed to vanish into my adulthood. So for days I retreated into my memories and felt sorry for myself, making every person and creature that cared about me uncomfortable with my misery until apparently Ty, my African grey, had had enough.

Ty asked clearly and simply in my own exasperated voice, "Why are you so grumpy?"

"Why are you so grumpy" was something I often said right after Ty took a swing at me. Usually I was about to lose a chunk of flesh because I was grumpy, not the bird. If I weren't so sullen, I probably would be paying closer attention to whether or not I was doing something to deserve to be bitten. So it was an ironic phrase in general, but a perfectly good question for the moment. Still, he had never said this before and it startled me.

I sat down in front of his cage, wondering if I had heard him right and when he asked again, I told him why I was grumpy. I explained what and who I had lost. I told him all the stories of bird ruckus that I could remember. Ty had asked and I needed to tell. I didn't care that he was a parrot and didn't understand; he laughed when I laughed and that was enough.

And when I was finished giggling and crying I was left with the realization that the stories were mine to keep. I realized that if my words rang back from one grey parrot, then maybe they rang back from everything I touched. What else would Ty say? What more would be told? Maybe stories lived forever and maybe in this one my grandparents did too. And come to think of it, maybe my life was destined to be one long bird ruckus. Wouldn't my grandparents be pleased?

The behaviors you shape and adore with your parrot may last a lifetime. Shape what you love and enjoy them.

2

Training Basics

The information in this chapter will form the basis for all training techniques presented in the rest of the book. Understanding the basic concepts of operant conditioning is important to having consistent success training and to building a relationship with your parrot. You do not have to understand these terms as well as a psychologist does, but if you comprehend them well enough to apply them they will quickly make more sense to you. As with any other skill, some people seem to have a natural rhythm for understanding how to cue, mark an event, reward, and shape behavior. Others of us do not, but all of us can practice and get better. So start practicing with positive reinforcement!

The best way to train a parrot is through positive reinforcement.

Positive Reinforcement

Positive reinforcement is the presentation of a stimulus following a behavior that serves to maintain or increase the frequency of that behavior. Simply put, it is training through rewards. Giving the reward increases the likelihood the subject will perform the desired behavior. Positive reinforcers (rewards) are usually something the learner finds enjoyable and pleasant; in parrots, a small piece of food is the usual reinforcer. When using positive reinforcement in training, the learner tends to exceed the effort necessary to obtain the reward. The best way to train a parrot is through positive reinforcement. Certainly all means of training, even punishment, can work. They just don't work as well and are not as much fun.

In her landmark book *Don't Shoot the Dog*, Karen Pryor notes that an interesting thing happened when trainers across continents and training different species began to use positive reinforcement as a sole means of shaping behavior. Everything from bears to horses to fish have demonstrated intelligence, enthusiasm, and curiosity in their training sessions when positive reinforcement was used. It turned out dolphins, which had been trained with positive reinforcement for decades, weren't the only playful intelligent animals. All animals exhibit more creativity and interest when they have the opportunity to puzzle out what they are being asked to do and when they are anticipating something good at the finish line.

Negative Reinforcement

Negative reinforcement is the removal of a stimulus following a behavior that serves to maintain or increase the frequency of that behavior. It is often called avoidance training. The learner will work only as hard as is necessary to avoid the stimulus, which is generally unpleasant. Parrots can learn behaviors this way, but it isn't recommended. An example would be holding up a towel or some other frightening object to herd a parrot into the crate. When the parrot goes into the crate, the towel disappears. The parrot will go in to avoid this stimulus, but you've probably eroded your relationship. It is also easy to overdo negative reinforcement and cause big problems. Aggression, escape behaviors, a lack of engagement, and fear behaviors can be created with the use of negative reinforcement.

There are instances when negative reinforcement works and has little repercussion. All the same, an animal will do only the bare minimum necessary to make whatever is being presented that he dislikes go away. In comparison, if you train with positive reinforcement instead, the bird will go into the crate just because he has a history of being rewarded for doing so. If there is no treat, he may be puzzled but then might offer another behavior, perhaps walking farther into the cage or coming back out and going back in again in an effort to elicit the treat. The potential for a reward creates enthusiasm and encourages creativity.

Punishment

Punishment is the presentation of an aversive stimulus or removal of a positive

Do I Have to Use "Good" as an Event Marker?

If appropriately and consistently used, any sound will work for an event marker. If you are using a word, a short easy word is best. Your parrot does not actually know what "good" means until you explain it to him by pairing it with a reward. And even then he is not going to get the actual meaning. To him "good" means "Here comes a treat!" You can use any word you want, even "bad." However, for your sake, using a word that makes sense to you and is something you will automatically say when pleased will make training much easier.

reinforcer that serves to reduce the frequency of a behavior. Punishment can be things like flicking a bird's beak, shaking his cage, dropping him to the floor, or even blowing in his face. It is something that is done to the bird that the bird dislikes and will seek to avoid through other behaviors. Punishment can sometimes stop undesirable behaviors, but often at the cost of a good relationship.

Punishment is tricky because in order for it to be understood it has to be administered

The only punishment you should use with your parrot is the time out procedure—turning your back on him for a few seconds.

at the exact moment the undesirable behavior is occurring. Let's say your parrot is screaming and you walk into the room to go shake his cage. You enter the room, so he stops screaming. At this point, to his mind shaking the cage is the result of his sitting quietly. Your bird will be confused and may become distrustful. The other thing that is tricky is that because dogs and people understand when we yell "No" or give them a dirty look, we think that this will work with our birds. However, you have actually previously taught your dog that "No" and a dirty look may mean he is about to be put outside. Without pairing your signs of disapproval with punishment and timing that punishment correctly the process will not work.

So perhaps the biggest danger of punishment is that if you do not use it precisely you create fear, aggression, and avoidance behavior in your parrot. Why risk it? If you make a mistake using positive reinforcement, your parrot may get a bit frustrated, but he is not going to distrust you and fear you. You can't lose using positive reinforcement.

Time Out

The only punishment that is important to have in your training arsenal is the removal of positive reinforcement. This is a "time out," but it isn't quite the same as the time out we use with our kids. You don't have to put your parrot back in his cage for 20 minutes. All you have to do is turn your back, walk away, or stop scratching his head for a few seconds. When I am training a parrot and it lunges at me, I put my treat hand down and look away. When the bird is no longer exhibiting aggressive behavior, I make eye contact and bring my hand back up. If your time out happens in conjunction with the lunge, it is a clear communication that this behavior removes the opportunity to get a treat. If the parrot wants a treat, over time (sometimes in just one training session) he will stop presenting the unwanted behavior.

With the exception of time outs, positive reinforcement can always be used more effectively with a parrot than punishment or negative reinforcement. And even time outs need to be paired with positive reinforcement in order to be effective. So now that you have an overview of these concepts, let's focus on the positive and talk about rewarding!

Using Positive Reinforcers (Rewarding)

Reinforcement is the key to making any behavior repeated. No behavior occurs consistently if there is not some form of pleasure or means of avoiding pain in performing it. This concept is the key to understanding how to shape behaviors. If you want to a behavior to be repeated, you have to reward it. If you never act excited or pleased when your husband brings you flowers, he will stop bringing you flowers. Certainly he bought them imagining your smile and how happy you would be with him. He was hoping for positive reinforcement. If he never gets it, he will quit trying with this behavior. The same is true of parrot behavior. If your parrot never gets anyone's attention or any kind of reaction when he calls out "Hello" he will stop saying it eventually. What's the point if no one in your flock is going to play along? If you want your parrot to do something you have to make sure there is a reward for that particular something.

However, it is important to understand that reinforcing a behavior has to be much more precise than simply rewarding. In order for reinforcement to work it has to be connected to the behavior. Your parrot steps up on your hand, he immediately gets a treat. In the bird's mind, stepping up equals a reward. The only way you can make an animal understand what it is being rewarded for is to have the reinforcement occur simultaneously with the behavior. You can also mark the event and reward it after the event occurs (we'll get to that in just a moment in the Event Marker section), but it is critical that your bird understands exactly what you are rewarding.

Another element that is critical to positive reinforcement's being effective is consistency. When you first train a behavior, it is important that you reward every time during your training session.

You will need to develop cues for each behavior you want to train. These can be verbal or physical or both.

If you only occasionally reward the behavior, forget to reward at first and then reward late, or accidentally reward early you will confuse and frustrate the bird. Sometimes an animal will cling to a behavior that has been accidentally rewarded, presenting it again and again, then becoming agitated and even aggressive when you do not reward it again. The bird is certain he is doing what you asked and thinks that you are not holding up your end of the bargain. This can make for a frustrating training session for everyone and set you back. Remember when you train that your parrot is trying to figure out what he is being rewarded for, and the clearer you are about it the faster he will learn.

Cues

When you are working on a behavior with your parrot it is important that you establish a cue. Cues can be verbal or physical, and if you want you can use both. For example if you are training your parrot to step onto your hand you might use both the cue of holding out your hand and of saying "Up." I like to use both a verbal and physical cue when I am training. Physical cues such as hand signals can

How Long is a Training Session?

The duration of a training session depends on a number of factors. First remember that every interaction is a training session. Don't miss out on opportunities to reward behaviors you enjoy and appreciate. When you are trying to train something specific, however, such as a trick, keep your training sessions short. You should try to always end a session before you lose your parrot's attention. This may be only a few minutes and is rarely longer than 15 minutes. However, you can pick up whenever your parrot is interested again, sometimes in an hour or so.

be minimized eventually to such small motions that it is hard for people to see that the bird is being cued in some way. This can be fun when you have dinner parties, especially if your parrot laughs on cue. We will talk a little more about establishing cues when we get to training specific behaviors, but in most cases you present the cue, give the parrot a short amount of time to respond, and reward him when he responds appropriately.

Take care that you do not repeat a cue over and over while you wait for your parrot to respond appropriately. I forget myself on occasion, asking again and again for a behavior because I am certain the parrot is going to offer it any second. Cue the parrot two or three times and if you are not getting a response, turn your back on him for a minute and then ask again. When this is a new behavior, go back to the last step in training the behavior where he was responding quickly. For example, if you were training him to fly to you and were calling him to your hand from three feet away, you might take a few steps closer to where he can hop onto your hand. Set him up to succeed and move forward from there. If he repeatedly ignores the cue, give him something simple to do, end the session, and try again later. When you frequently reward your bird for behaviors you cued ten times before he finally responded correctly, he will learn to respond only after you have asked over and over. After all, that must be what you wanted. You trained it!

You should also not wait for more than five seconds or so for a response once your parrot has learned that response, less if you want an instant response. The

One of the best event markers is a clicker. It does not take a parrot long to learn that the click means a reward is on the way.

problem with rewarding after a long wait is that you teach your bird that even if he takes his sweet time responding, he can still get a reward. This is called training latency, and it is an easy trap to fall into. Be precise with your cue.

Event Marker

While it is important to reinforce a behavior as it is occurring, this is not always practical. Let's say you are trying to get your parrot to whistle the theme to *Doctor Who* but don't want to reward him until he whistles the first six notes in succession. If you hang out waiting to reward him until he does it right, you may be out in front of the cage with a peanut in your hand for a month or more. Your savior in this situation and a tool you should always use when training is an event marker. An event marker—also called a bridge or a bridging stimulus—is a sound that is used to inform an animal that it just did what you wanted and a treat is forthcoming. An event marker is a critical tool for anyone who wants to better communicate with an animal. It allows you to reward behavior the moment it is occurring. So go do the laundry or check your Facebook page and then when you finally hear your parrot whistle *Doctor Who* from the other room, you can call out "good" as an event marker. Then go give him a treat. If your bird always hears "good" before he is given a treat, then he will understand that this whistle gets him a reward. If you don't use an event marker, by the time you get in the room with a treat your parrot will have moved on to another behavior and you may reward something undesirable, like the sound of the fire alarm or your husband snoring.

Two Recommended Event Markers

It does not take long for a parrot to learn what an event marker means, but if you have never used one before, you will have to teach him. If you are using a clicker, click and hand him a treat a few times and he will start to associate the sound with a treat. At first, the clicker may startle your bird, so you want him to associate the sound with a treat as quickly as possible. You can also just use the word "good" and try it out a couple of times with your parrot before you start working on a behavior, or just dive in. Your parrot may not quite get it at first, but pretty soon he will come to associate the word "good" with the experience of being handed a treat.

For some parrots, a head scratch or a cuddle is just as good a reward as an edible treat.

Timing and Precision

Like everything else in training, your event marker needs to be very precise. It is important that you mark the behavior right when it happens. And if it is a behavior that takes several seconds to perform, like whistling the theme to *Doctor Who*, you need to take care to wait until the behavior is completed before you mark the event. If you say "good" or click too soon you may accidentally teach the parrot to truncate the behavior, and it will be difficult to undo this.

The timing of marking the event also includes the length of the event marker itself. If you use "good" as an event marker it should be a quick, clipped, and precise word. Say "good," not "gooooooood," as if you are someone training in slow motion. The word "good" should also be calm and controlled. I've certainly had my moments when I got overly excited that the parrot I was training got it. Trust me, shrieking "good" and spontaneously dancing may not be reinforcing to the parrot. (Although if you

When your parrot makes a breakthrough in training, consider offering a jackpot—a huge and unexpected reward.

are training parrots at a workshop your audience might be highly amused.) Clickers are fabulous because they consist of one short click every time you press the button. So if you have trouble keeping your event marker short, sweet, and free of excess emotion you may want to try training with a clicker.

Variable Reinforcement

When you first start training a behavior, it is important to reward every time you use an event marker. Until your parrot is consistently presenting the behavior without hesitation, you should reward every time. Constant reinforcement, however, is necessary only at the learning stage. Once your parrot has it down, it is time to start varying the reinforcement.

If an animal is given the same reward every time he is asked and then performs a behavior, soon that behavior will get more and more mechanical; if you do not reinforce it a couple of times he will stop doing it. So if you are worried that using positive reinforcement means constantly giving treats for every little thing, stop worrying. Not only do you not need to give out treats every single time once the bird has learned the behavior, it is important that you do not do so.

A schedule of variable reinforcement means that the animal is rewarded at random. Perhaps you reward the behavior the third time and the sixth time it is performed. Your parrot will start wondering when that treat is coming, and because it comes at random there is a level of excitement. Every time might or

Help! My Parrot Has Amnesia

Sometimes when you are working on a training a behavior, for no apparent reason your parrot will seem to completely forget what you were working on. It will be as if he has never heard the cue before even though you are right in the middle of a training session. Don't get frustrated. This happens to all of us. There is nothing wrong with you or your parrot. Your parrot could just be distracted or maybe confused. Take a few steps back in training to the last place where your parrot was doing really well and seemed to understand what you were training. See if you can get one or two repetitions and end the training session on a positive note. You can come back to training when your parrot has more focus later.

You will need to break down each behavior into small steps for your parrot to learn.

might not be treat time. Vary how often you reward, the treats you offer, and how much of a treat you give. If your parrot never knows whether there will be a treat or whether it will be a peanut or a sunflower seed this time, he won't have the opportunity to decide he doesn't feel like waving for a sunflower seed. He might get a sunflower seed but next time he will probably get something different.

The success of casinos and lotteries is entirely because of variable reinforcement. If I won $1 every time I bought a $1 lottery ticket, I would probably make less and less of an effort to stop off at the gas station and buy a ticket on draw days. And if after winning $1 every time two tickets in a row were losers, I would probably stop playing altogether. However, I win $1 only every month or so, and last week I won $10! I keep playing because I just might win. In fact I might just hit the jackpot, which is another great training tool to have in your bag of tricks.

Jackpot

A jackpot is a very useful training tool that comes as a surprise and makes the possibilities of reward even grander for an animal. This is a reward that is huge, maybe ten times the size of a normal treat. It should be unexpected but works particularly well if given when your parrot has a breakthrough in training and the session is ended. This conveys a clear message and also may cement the moment in the parrot's memory. Who wouldn't remember and try to repeat something that got them a gigantic reward?

A jackpot doesn't have to be a handful of treats, however. It can be anything that the parrot considers wonderful and he does not get very often. Maybe this is an immediate trip in his cage to hang out on the porch on a sunny day. Maybe it's a ride in the car. (It's weird, but there is just about nothing my Senegal parrot loves more than to go for a drive.) Or perhaps the jackpot is just half of a pomegranate and permission to stain anything within five feet of the feast. Whatever it is, giving your parrot a jackpot at the right moment will make training fun and exciting.

Successive Approximations

Hopefully now you understand how important timing and consistency are in training. Using a cue, event marker, and reinforcement requires taking care to communicate clearly about your requests and what it takes to get a reward. As you begin to train you will start to see that even the simplest behavior actually requires training a series of behaviors, several steps that need to be understood in order to get to the final result. These steps are called approximations.

An approximation is breaking down a desired behavior into small steps. Each approximation must be learned before moving on to the next step. The end result is that all these steps together become the final behavior. Approximations are used to shape a behavior. For example, imagine you are training your parrot to step onto your hand. The steps might be:

1. Parrot faces you.
2. Parrot reaches for a treat.
3. Reaches for a treat over your hand.
4. Reaches for treat and lifts up a foot.
5. Reaches for treat, lifts up foot, and puts that foot onto your hand.

6. All of the above and parrot puts weight on the foot on your hand.
7. All of the above and parrot puts both feet on your hand.
8. Parrot does all of the above and stands upright on your hand.
9. Parrot does all of the steps and stands in a relaxed stance with all his weight on your hand.

All these steps equal stepping up onto your hand, but in training you will ask for each of these steps one at a time, building on the others. Each approximation is marked and rewarded when you get the response you request. When the bird presents the behavior without hesitation and understands what he is getting rewarded for, then you move on to the next step. If he gets it, he will wonder why this time he didn't get rewarded and stretch a little farther to get the reward for the next step.

Take note of your parrot's body language, looking for signs of hesitation such as leaning away, craning his neck, and similar behaviors.

The wonderful thing about training in successive approximations is that when an animal learns that this is the way training works he will become creative. You will find your bird offering behaviors, trying to figure out what the next step is, using his brain and having fun. If you go too fast and he gets confused, however, you can relax your criteria and go back down the list to an early step. Training this way works for all behaviors. By using positive reinforcement and successive approximations, you can shape just about any behavior.

Shaping

Shaping involves using small steps and slowly molding a behavior from the beginning to the end. Training using shaping is clearer to the bird, allowing him to understand each component of training before moving on to the next step. When using approximations to shape a behavior, you should take care that you do not choose steps that are too hard or too easy for the subject you are training. A parrot who doesn't understand what you are asking will get frustrated and quit the session. Conversely, a parrot that already knows what's next and is being held back may have a shortened attention span and also stop working. So how do you make sure you are training with the right expectations and at the right speed?

The best first step is to have a clear idea of how you are going to break the behavior you want to train into small parts. This is setting your criteria. Writing the parts down as steps is ideal. Break them into the smallest components you can imagine, like those listed in the step up training outlined above and then adjust how quickly you go from one step to the next based on the parrot's behavior. There are many right ways to train any behavior, and I will keep reminding you of this as we talk about training various different things. You may think of a way that is easier for you than what I outline. The important thing is that what you outline works for you and your bird and that you stick to it.

Know what step you are on and reward only for that criterion. If you change your mind about what you are going to reward part way in you will confuse your poor parrot. Don't hold out a treat and then decide to make the parrot come a little farther even though he has already met the criterion. Be honest and trustworthy. Don't tease, taunt, bait, or change the rules on your parrot.

You should go to the next step when the parrot performs the current step without hesitation. If you are training a step up and your parrot is putting a foot onto your hand but quickly pulling it off and stepping away from you, he is not ready to be asked to move to the next step. He is hesitating. Look for the subtle body language because that is the way a parrot communicates. Leaning away, craning his neck to take the treat while keeping his body away from you, and skittering away to a safer distance after performing the approximation you requested are all signs of being hesitant. Be patient with your parrot and with yourself, move forward in small steps, and have fun!

Confused? A Simple Recap

If you have never trained an animal before, this chapter might have been a lot of information to take in all at once. Do not let it all intimidate you. You may have to go back and re-read it a few times once you start training, but these concepts will

Parrots trained through the use of successive approximations will try out new behaviors in an effort to figure out the next step on their own.

Attention Please!

An important thing to remember with a cue is that there is no reason to use it if your parrot is not paying attention. This is one of the most common mistakes that animal trainers make. How many times have you seen someone screaming for a dog to come that is two blocks away and obviously not paying any attention? Cuing doesn't work if your animal isn't listening, and cuing when a parrot is obviously distracted can teach him to ignore you. Whenever you are about to cue your parrot, first look to see whether he has finished the last treat you gave him and is looking at you waiting for what's next. If he is engaged and ready, then give him the cue. If you cannot get your parrot to look at you and pay attention at all, you should wrap up the training session.

start to make sense as you put them to work. Chances are you already use some of these tools in your everyday life. You just need to pay attention and become mindful of using them.

The important concepts you need to take away from this chapter are that operant conditioning using positive reinforcement is the most effective way to train, have fun, and build a positive relationship with any animal. This means that your parrot is invited to participate and if he does, he gets a reward. Your parrot has a choice whether or not he wishes to get a treat.

The process of training with positive reinforcement involves a cue, an event marker, and a reward. For example you might say "Step up" and hold out your hand as a cue. When your parrot steps up, you will mark the event by saying "good." Then you follow "good" with handing your bird a treat. Using this process you can shape a behavior that is new to the parrot. Remember these concepts and the rest will make more sense the more practice you have. And if you already have experience training with positive reinforcement, then brush up and let's look at training good behavior!

The Devil Wears Prada Knockoffs

Ty, my African grey parrot, used to pay attention to my shoes. When I walked into the room he would look first at my feet and then at my face. If I had my hiking boots on we were up to business as usual, but if I had on high heels he was a different bird. He would puff up to five times his normal slick size, sway like a snake, and growl, "See you later, alligator." It was intriguing. It was funny. It was my favorite parlor trick. I would demonstrate it over cocktails for friends modeling various styles of shoes, my high heels always greeted with the same venom. We all laughed except for Ty.

   I thought that my bird looked at my shoes to decide whether I was leaving, and that high heels indicated a long absence. I thought he was mad at me for leaving him. I didn't understand yet that an African grey is a perfect funhouse mirror, sending your reflection back at you only larger than life.

   My world was in chaos the second and third year of Ty's life. I was running a business that was as ego-bruising as it was time-consuming. My friends can tell you stories that make my years as a process server (mostly serving evictions) sound like a great plot to a successful comedy. These were the stories that I told. What I remember now are the stories that I didn't share, tales that would actually make a good indie movie with a gut-wrenching ending. It was cluttered, shadowy, and sad where I served papers—and what I saw of the world was furious with me.

   The hardest days were meeting these people in court, their wrinkled clothes, ragged anger, and accusations pitted against my high heels and perfect enunciation. In court, I was the devil.

I hated being the devil. I hated slipping my high heels on to go to court. When I was in a depressed neighborhood, even wearing jeans and tennis shoes, I could still feel those high heels rubbing blisters at the base of my toes, clicking on the pavement, announcing that I didn't belong. I put it out of my mind, though, and told myself I was only working. It was just a job.

Ty saw something that would take me another year to recognize. Ty saw it in my body language and heard it in the inflection of my voice. I hated those high heels, and had I listened to my tenacious grey alter ego, I would have realized that my parrot wasn't mad at me at all, but that when I put on heels I was furious with myself. Ty read my body language perfectly. It was only when I started listening to the parrot listening to me that I realized what I really wanted to do with my life. And once I started training birds for living, he stopped noticing my shoes. Behavior and training creates an amazing connection with the animals that share your home.

3

Just Make My Parrot Behave!

Even if you decide you do not want to spend a lot of time training your parrot to do tricks, the better you understand the theory of training and how to apply it, the easier it will be for you to maintain desired behavior and avoid undesirable behaviors from your parrot. The reason I don't just say "good" or "bad" behavior is because those terms can be very subjective. Something that makes you miserable might not bother someone else in the least. I spend a lot of time writing at my computer and have a low tolerance for loud repetitive noises. My parrots are not silent, but the noises they make do not bother me most of the time. I know plenty of people, however, who can tune out the sound of a parrot imitating the fire alarm, something I would find undesirable. Of course, there are some obvious behaviors that are undesirable, such as attacking or biting. So translate desirable and undesirable into what makes the most sense in your home. You have to live with your parrot, not me!

Applied Behavior Analysis

We talked about operant conditioning in the previous chapter, and applied behavior analysis is essentially taking the concept of operant conditioning and breaking it down in order to analyze and have an effect on behavior. Applied behavior analysis was described by B.F. Skinner as having three parts. There is the occasion in which the behavior occurs, the behavior itself, and the consequence. All of these work together, and behavior never occurs without there being an antecedent or a consequence. It is not independent. So if you can change any of these three components you can adjust behavior. Let's look at these three concepts; they are critical for understanding how we shape behavior—many times without even meaning to do so. We will come back to these concepts in sections where changing behavior is being discussed.

Antecedent

The antecedent consists of the stimuli, events, and conditions that immediately precede a behavior. The antecedent does not cause the behavior to happen, but it does set the stage for the behavior to occur. Antecedents do not *cause* a particular behavior—your parrot can still make a decision about how to react—but they do increase or decrease the likelihood a behavior will occur. For example,

Understanding applied behavior analysis will make training your parrot easier.

if you hold up a stick for your parrot to step onto he may step up onto it if he previously has had positive experiences doing so. He also may run away when he sees the stick if he has had negative experiences with it. Presenting the stick is the antecedent that sets the behavior in motion. So if you have a parrot that has been trained to step up onto a stick, holding a stick in front of him will increase the likelihood that he will step up.

Behavior

Behavior is what your parrot (or any other organism) does that can be observed. Flapping wings, pinning pupils—rapidly contracting and expanding the pupils, usually a sign of excitement or aggression, climbing down from perches, and whistling are all observable behaviors. This may seem obvious to you, but it is

Experiencing a positive consequence—such as a scratch on the head—for a behavior makes it more likely the parrot will repeat that behavior.

important to define. Animal trainers and parrot owners back themselves into a corner by forgetting that the actual behavior is the only thing that can be observed. What an animal is thinking or feeling is not a measureable behavior. Since you cannot measure thinking and feeling and really cannot define them, it is impractical to try to shape and change feelings and thoughts. Yet we frequently try.

People ask me how they can train their parrot not to be so grumpy or teach their bird not to be so neurotic. Or they might say that their parrot is jealous of their spouse. None of these things are observable behaviors in and of themselves; they are are emotions. Because these are inner states of being and not behaviors, you cannot work to change them. Feelings and thoughts are elusive, but you can focus on the measurable behaviors and shape them. You can strategize how to increase or decrease behaviors such as how many times a day your boyfriend calls or how loudly your wife yells at you. So keep in mind that guessing what is going on in your parrot's head is a fun pastime and a great conversation to have with friends, but it will not help you train your bird.

Consequences

Consequences are the stimuli, events, and conditions that happen after a behavior occurs. Consequences are important because they dictate the likelihood of whether or not a behavior will repeat itself. There are many different consequences that affect a parrot's behavior, and some of them are rather subtle. Social interaction such as a scratch on the head, a vocal response, or even just a housemate walking into the room can be a positive consequence.

Responding to consequences is nature's way of continuing a species. Parrots in the wild have close calls and brushes with danger all the time. A parrot that pauses to consider an approaching hawk while all his buddies shout out alarms and head for the hills may quickly find that he is on the menu. After being chased and escaping, he will not repeat the behavior of sitting still immediately following the antecedent of an alarm call. It works for encouraging behavior too. Imagine a parrot finding a hard-shelled nut he has never seen before in the wild and going through the trouble of cracking it open. If he finds something tasty inside, the next time he finds nuts like that he will be more likely to break it open. While they may not be life or death situations, consequences work to increase or decrease the probability of a behavior's being repeated in your home.

Putting it all Together

Understanding the building blocks of applied behavior analysis can help you see why your parrot repeats certain appealing or annoying behaviors in your home. Coming back to these basics will help you whenever you are dealing with problem behaviors and more importantly help you keep the good behavior repeating. The most basic training is maintaining and shaping everyday behaviors in your home.

Now that you understand that there

Anthropomorphism

Anthropomorphism is the act of applying human traits to an animal. When you tell someone that your parrot is feeling guilty because he bit you, this is anthropomorphism. You are making the assumption that your parrot is displaying the human trait of feeling guilty. While animals certainly have emotions, the act of making assumptions that they are acting based on human feelings is detrimental to training and solving behavior problems.

is an antecedent that sets up a behavior and a consequence that dictates whether or not it will repeat, think about this in your daily interactions. There are so many simple everyday things we reward and encourage. Most of them are enjoyable and create behaviors we love. After sixteen years with my African grey parrot Ty, he has a bevy of behaviors he has learned and repeats because he gets a response. He asks for apples, peanuts, and almonds by name and correctly because I have rewarded his speaking of those words with the correlating food:

- Antecedent: I walk by with an apple.
- Behavior: Ty says, "apple".
- Consequence: Ty gets a piece of apple.

Sometimes the rewards are much less obvious in the training as well. Ty belches when I walk by with a beer because he has almost always gotten a response out of me:

- Antecedent: I walk by with a beer.
- Behavior: Ty belches.
- Consequence: I gasp or giggle or glare at him; he gets attention.

It's a rude behavior, but I've rewarded it just by reacting. And I guess I think it is a little bit funny or I wouldn't keep reacting to it. This is an example of a behavior that might be undesirable in someone else's home but is just fine in your own.

And Ty has trained me too. He lifts his wings if he wants to be cuddled. He is rather standoffish, but I know he will let me cuddle him if he is willing to lift up his wings. If he pulls his wings tight, forget it—you better not bother him. So I have always tested the water first. Now he solicits some quality interaction with wings up. This is how the training works on me:

- Antecedent: Ty lifts his wings up.
- Behavior: I reach out and cuddle him.
- Consequence: Ty fluffs up his feathers and preens me.

Even if you do not spend a lot of time training tricks, these are the sorts of things that we train daily, and being mindful of them makes everyday living with a parrot a real pleasure. Personally, there is nothing I love more than realizing I have just been had, that a parrot has trained me. I get more joy out of that than some of the fun things I have trained parrots to do. After all, living happily with your parrot is the most important thing. So how do you get started teaching these good behaviors and learning to communicate? You start by training your parrot to engage, play, and accept new situations. You start with socializing.

Socializing

Understanding that all animals are products of their experience, if you are bringing a new parrot into your home it is a good idea to expose your bird to as many experiences as possible. Of course, you want to make sure that these experiences are positive. Parrots that have positive experiences with trying new food, playing with new toys, going different places, and meeting new people are more open and interested in engaging in new experiences. Of course all parrots are individuals and some birds are more

Parrots exposed to a variety of foods, toys, and other experiences when young are more likely to be eager to try new things when they are older.

withdrawn than others, but overall this is a good foundation to build for a parrot.

If you have a very young parrot, less than a year old, it is especially important that you allow your parrot to experience the world. Young animals have a window of time during which they are little sponges, taking in as many experiences as possible to figure out their world and how to survive in it. It is not impossible to teach an old parrot new tricks; all the same, it is easier to teach a young one. Parrots that have been exposed to a variety of foods and toys at a young age are often more likely to be willing to test out new treats and experiment with playthings in their environment when they are older. Plus, it is just plain fun to watch a young parrot discovering a world of possibilities.

Giving your parrot an opportunity to meet people of all shapes and sizes can be a great thing. Just take a tremendous amount of care that such meetings are on your parrot's terms. When new people come into the house, give them treats to drop into your parrot's bowl or to hand to the parrot if he is willing to reach out for a treat from a stranger. If your parrot and your human visitor are both comfortable

Learned Helplessness

Learned helplessness is a very effective means to creating a passive animal but a very unfortunate way of doing it. It occurs when an animal is not allowed to escape a situation it finds very frightening. It is basically forcing an animal to just "get over it." If a parrot is frightened of a person—lunging, biting, and trying to escape—and this person grabs him and holds him until he no longer tries to escape, this creates learned helplessness. The parrot remains passive and if given an opportunity to escape or lunge at the person, he does not. He has given up as if he is helpless. It is more than just this, however. Animals in a state of learned helplessness may exhibit depression and emotional problems; they may even be more prone to sickness. The way to combat learned helplessness is to give animals the opportunities to make decisions and control their world. It is the little things like choosing whether or not to step up or come out of the cage that will give your parrot a busy mind and a zest for life. If you train your parrot with positive reinforcement, he will almost always choose to step up when asked, but the important thing is that he gets to choose!

Introduce new people to your parrot as often as possible so that he becomes well socialized.

with it, have your parrot step up for the visitor. Try to make sure that nothing scary happens. If your visitor is not comfortable and drops your parrot thinking he is going to bite him or her, your parrot may lose confidence in strangers.

You can take socializing one step further and take your parrot on trips to the pet store, parrot clubs, or friends' houses as well. The experience of seeing new places, meeting new people, and having a highly interactive world can be wonderful for encouraging curiosity and molding a well-adjusted parrot. Of course, this level of socialization is not without risks. Things may happen that frighten your parrot or are even dangerous in environments that are out of your control. It is possible you could also expose your parrot to diseases as well. So how far you take you socializing is really up to you; stay within your comfort zone.

Some amount of socialization is critical. People will visit your home, and someone will have to care for your parrot when you are away. There is also the possibility of

When introducing your parrot to a child, supervise the interaction carefully and reward your parrot for staying calm.

new roommates and new significant others in your life. So a parrot that is comfortable with strangers and new situations will be less likely to exhibit undesirable behavior when these situations arise. However, if you do not plan on taking your parrot with you on frequent outings, you do not have to go the extra mile to expose your parrot to everything possible. It's your life. Make it work for you.

So how exactly do you socialize a parrot? Embrace opportunities to introduce new people. If your best friend has a ten-year-old daughter and your parrot has never seen a child before, invite parent and child over. Explain to the girl that your parrot may be frightened and that she needs to move slowly and follow your instructions. Then watch your parrot closely. If the moment the little girl walks into the room your parrot moves to the back of the cage and growls or shrieks, keep her far away from the cage until your parrot is comfortable. Once the parrot is sitting calmly, let the girl step closer to the parrot, giving the parrot a treat each time she gets closer and the parrot doesn't react. The parrot should also be stepped up only if he is completely comfortable. Your goal is for your parrot to come out of the experience thinking, "Hey, that was kind of fun and I even got a treat." Next time he sees a ten-year-old girl (or a person who resembles one to the parrot), he will be expecting a similar outcome. If all your parrot's experiences with people are similar you will have a well-socialized parrot.

Training to Play

Comfort with new experiences and people is very important basic training. This will lay the groundwork for being able to train a large variety of behaviors. Your parrot will be more likely to be well adjusted and unperturbed by changes in his environment or new challenges. Another important set of traits to encourage with basic training is your parrot's interest in his surroundings and curiosity. A curious, playful parrot is easier to train and more likely to present desirable behaviors because he knows how to entertain himself.

In the wild, parrots are constantly exploring and investigating their environment. A busy parrot is a happy parrot! Wild parrots, however, have a lifetime of positive reinforcement from making the effort to investigate. Foraging and exploring yield new tastes and proper nutrition. They are also ways to find interesting things to destroy and examine. The parrot has been rewarded for his efforts. If your parrot has always had a bowl of food in front of him and the same old toys in his cage, he may not have learned to explore and play. This inquisitiveness has not been trained, but it is not too late to train it.

Presenting your parrot's food in different ways—such as hanging on a kabob—encourages him to try new foods.

Playing with Food

It may be rude when people do it, but you definitely want your parrot to learn to play with his food. A balanced diet involves a lot more than just some pellets and seeds. All the same, you can give your parrot all the vegetables in the world, but if he doesn't touch them he is never going to benefit from their nutrition. Some parrots are picky eaters, of course, but trying out new foods is something a parrot needs to learn to do, and you can teach him.

The first thing that can make new food items interesting is just to mix them up. Most fruits and vegetables that are good for you are good for your parrot too. Consult with your vet about foods that are poisonous, but outside of those few items, put everything but the kitchen sink into your parrot's bowl. Broccoli, carrots, grapes, apples, cooked sweet potatoes, green beans, corn—you name it—put a piece of those foods in the bowl. If it is a mixed-up pile your parrot may be enticed to pick through it and maybe try out a bite or two. Teach your bird that there are all kinds of things that might be in his bowl and it is worth investigating. If he won't investigate a bowl full of veggies (behavior), then you need to change either the antecedent (food arrives in a bowl) or the consequence (end result is fun and tasty).

You can see whether changing the antecedent helps by changing the presentation of the food. Maybe your parrot would be more likely to investigate food in other shapes and places than just in the bowl. Try hanging a bit of corncob with a skewer or with a zip tie. Shove broccoli stalks through the bars of the cage or weave leafy greens through the bars. String up apple, pear, carrot and other crunchy bits together so your parrot might be encouraged to try out each.

You Have to Live with It

Sometimes when I am giving a lecture or doing a workshop someone in the audience will tell me about how they squirt their parrot with water to get him to stop screaming. This person understands that this is negative and dares me to tell her that she is a bad person. The thing is, I won't. Is it the best way to train? No, it's not the way I would do it, but I don't have to live with your bird. I do not believe in making people feel bad about their training methds. Don't worry about being a perfect trainer. Don't worry about being a better parrot owner than other people. Worry about keeping the peace in your home and having an environment that you love.

If you adopt a parrot that is not used to playing with toys, you may need to encourage him. Reward him for investigating his toys until he learns that the toys themselves are fun to play with.

If your parrot is not enticed by spicing up the presentation, you can try making it more rewarding to investigate and play instead. Likely there are foods your parrot likes a great deal such as almonds, sunflower seeds, or pine nuts. Try shoving seeds into cooked squash or harder fruit so that he can see them but has to chew through the new food to get to what he thinks is rewarding. Bundle almonds inside leafy greens. Find new ways to make it rewarding to destroy, play with, and taste new food to get to the preferred and loved treats.

Playing with Toys

Teaching your parrot to play with the toys that are placed in his cage is a similar process. Some parrots are more playful than others, so you should not expect your parrot to be constantly chewing and banging toys around, but if your parrot completely ignores the toys in his cage you should do something to get him to be more interactive. Touching, chewing, exploring, and banging a toy are behaviors, so you can increase their likelihood of repeating by changing the antecedent or the consequence, just as with eating new food.

If your parrot is not playing with the toys in his cage, maybe he needs new toys. Animals tend to interact with the toys in their environments if they are changed fairly often. You should consider changing one or two of your parrot's toys every week. This doesn't mean they have to be brand new, but if you have a bunch of toys you rotate, whatever goes in is still something different for your bird. Try a variety of toys as well: those that can be chewed on and destroyed, those that are puzzles, and those that make noise. Change them up and see whether you can trigger your parrot to investigate.

Changing the antecedent may not be enough for a bird that has not had a lot of reinforcement for playing with toys. Maybe he just doesn't know how much joy there is in nibbling a piece of pine into a nub. When he figures it out he may find the playing reinforcing all by itself, but in the meantime you can help make it positive. When you see your parrot reach out and touch a new toy, give him a treat. Reward him for investigating and then reward him for chewing. If it is a puzzle toy, you can put treats inside where he can see them but has to work out how to get to them. If he doesn't immediately try, you can reward him for touching the toy until he is consistently touching and manipulating it, then ultimately rewarding himself.

A parrot that is well socialized and plays with his food and toys is less likely to find annoying ways, such as screaming, to get your attention. He is getting his own

Contrafreeloading

If giving your parrots treats for training makes you feel manipulative, consider the concept of contrafreeloading. Studies with animals have shown that animals will perform a learned response in order to get a treat even when that same food is readily available. For example, a chicken given the choice of eating from a bowl of corn nearby or pecking on piano keys to make corn appear will peck on the keys and eat that food. This experiment has been replicated with rodents, pigeons, cats, and even parrots. Animals, including humans, are built to behave rather than passively sit and observe. We want to interact with our environment and have some control over it, and training gives us this opportunity. So let your parrot puzzle out how to get that treat. Nobody wants to be a perch potato!

reward for behavior that you both appreciate. And all of this can be trained with the same concepts we will be using to train tricks. Even a well-adjusted parrot can pick up undesirable behaviors, however. So let's talk about bad behavior for a bit.

Oh No! Bad Behavior!

When your parrot is presenting undesirable behavior, applied behavior analysis and your notebook are your best friends. Remember that no behavior repeats itself without being reinforced and that every behavior has something that sets the stage for it to occur. This is true every time. There is something that occurs right before your parrot bites and something your parrot finds rewarding when he does bite, or the bite would not occur and occur repeatedly.

People frequently tell me that their parrots did something with no warning and for no reason. This is never true. If it were true then you may as well just give up; shaping behavior or controlling anything in your life would be impossible. Admittedly, it is sometimes very difficult to figure out what set up the behavior and how it is being rewarded, but that is where your notebook is critical. Put your guesses and your hurt feelings aside and start recording all of the details of every occurrence of the behavior you dislike. Eventually you will find there is a pattern.

Once you find the pattern you can shape the behavior by changing the conversation with your parrot. You can do this for every problem behavior.

Change the Antecedent

Sometimes the easiest way to deal with an undesirable behavior is to change what triggers it. This is not training so much as it is just not setting up the problem. Sometimes, just not triggering the problem behavior is the quickest solution. Even though you can train anything with positive reinforcement it can be a long and complicated endeavor. Changing the antecedent can be a valuable short-cut to the desired result.

Sometimes changing the antecedent to a behavior is the quickest solution. Your parrot can't fly up to your dining room chandelier if you keep him out of that room.

My mother once called me and explained she was having an issue with her cat attacking her whenever she made her bed. Myke would jump up on the bed, crawl under the sheet and jump at my mom with claws out. This did more than just make it difficult to get the sheets and bedspread in order—it also left my mom bleeding and unhappy. She asked me how she could train Myke to stop this very undesirable behavior, which the cat obviously found fun and rewarding.

- Antecedent: Mom shakes out sheet and pulls it to the top of bed.
- Behavior: Myke jumps up on bed
- Consequence: Myke get to play in sheets and swat at Mom.

My mom waited patiently expecting me to come up with a training plan, which I briefly considered doing. She could make the bed so slowly that there would be no reinforcement for the cat, no waving sheets or spaces to crawl under. With no reinforcement, the behavior would eventually extinguish. She could also train Myke to stay on a chair for treats. If Myke was sitting on a chair waiting for a reward, she couldn't also be in the bed wreaking havoc, but all of this sounded like a lot of work to me. So I said, "How about if you shut the door before you make the bed?"

My mom burst into laughter and I did too, but this was a very valid answer to the problem behavior. Change the antecedent. If the cat wasn't in the room when the bed was being made, the behavior would not be triggered. Or you could change the antecedent in the way that would work best in my house: just don't ever make your bed. Changing the antecedent is a very effective tool for problem-solving and one that is sometimes the least taxing and time consuming.

Of course sometimes the antecedent is out of our control or it is something that has to be performed without fail in your household, such as putting your parrot back into the cage. If your parrot bites you when you try to put him back in the cage, you could just leave him out all day long, but this is neither safe nor desirable. So if you can't change the antecedent you can instead look at the consequence.

Cage-Bound Birds

Parrots that do not have proper socialization and positive experiences with new activities may become cage-bound. A parrot that is cage-bound will not venture out of the cage even if you leave the door open all day long. Proper training can overcome this, and it is never too late to socialize a parrot, but it is still a sad situation. A parrot that is fearful of new things and people does not live an enriching life and is highly stressed. Stress can cause disease and start a pattern of feather-plucking. Your parrot should enjoy being in his cage but also enjoy the possibilities on the outside.

Training an incompatible behavior, such as whispering or sitting quietly, will help solve a screaming problem.

Change the Consequence

If before you go to work in the morning you put your parrot away and he bites you every time, and he sometimes bites you instead of stepping onto the perch, there is obviously a problem. You don't want to get bitten, of course, but you have to get your parrot into the cage so you can get to your job on time. Let's say that not letting the parrot out in the morning is not an option. Maybe you are like me and want your parrot(s) to be able to enjoy time out of the cage as much as possible. So what do you do?

The sequence that you want is that when you show your parrot the perch inside his cage, the behavior you get is that he steps up. In fact he used to do that. So what happened? A behavior that repeats itself has been reinforced, and one that stops repeating itself it is not being reinforced enough. So what is reinforcing about stepping up onto the perch inside the cage? Break down the behavior:

- Antecedent: Rebecca shows Ty the perch inside his cage.
- Behavior: Ty steps up onto the perch.
- Consequence: Rebecca shuts the cage door and leaves for work.

That's not very reinforcing at all, is it? Why would Ty consistently step up to be locked in the cage when there is nothing fun about it? Being outside the cage was much more reinforcing. So if you want your parrot to step up consistently, you will have to change the consequence. Try not feeding him his breakfast until you put him away and leave. A big bowl of goodies is worth stepping back into the cage for. Or maybe there is a new favorite toy or vegetables strewn about the cage to play with that were not there before. If you want repetition of the behavior to increase, improve the consequences. If you want the behavior not to repeat, you need to remove the positive consequences. An even better problem-solving technique is changing the consequence in conjunction with training an incompatible behavior.

Train an Incompatible Behavior

An incompatible behavior is something that an animal cannot do while doing the behavior you are trying to eliminate. For example, Myke the cat could not sit on a chair waiting for a treat and play in the bed at the same time. Do you have a parrot that attacks your feet? If you train your parrot to go to the top of his cage, he cannot go to the top of his cage and attack your feet at the same time. This is often an extremely helpful technique in shifting and shaping problem behaviors.

Training an incompatible behavior can be especially helpful with screaming. Generally speaking, screaming is all about contact and attention. It is a very easy to reinforce screaming because it is so hard to ignore it. A parrot that wants our attention and screams will eventually get us to break down and pay attention to him. The sequence usually goes like this:

- Antecedent: Rebecca leaves the room.
- Behavior: Ty screams.
- Consequence: Rebecca comes back into the room to tell him to be quiet.

If the behavior repeats and continues, it is being rewarded. So having a person return to the room must be rewarding in this instance. Ignoring the parrot will work to decrease the behavior and eventually extinguish it. However, there will be a lot of screaming in the meantime, and the parrot is still looking for a way to get attention. It will be much more effective to train your bird to get your attention in some other way while you ignore the screaming.

The parrot cannot scream and call out "Hello" at the same time. So if you start rewarding "Hello" and ignoring the screaming, you should hear many more friendly greetings and a lot less screaming parrot. You can reward with treats or just by answering back and popping into the room with the bird occasionally when he offers the behavior you want. Again, this is a conversation. Once you figure out what your parrot finds rewarding, you can offer the reward for the behavior you like instead of the behavior that bothers you. Your job is to make sure that the things you appreciate get rewarded; if you don't, your parrot will instead find annoying ways to get the attention that he wants.

All problem behaviors can be managed by understanding how behavior is set up and rewarded. Some are more complicated than others, and sometimes it is hard to see what is happening in your own home because we all have our own habits and quirks. With a foundation of applied behavior analysis and positive reinforcement, you can understand how these behaviors are shaped and work at shaping them on purpose instead of by accident.

We're All In This Together

As we move forward into learning how to purposefully train new behaviors, it is a good idea to consider everyone in the household. Every interaction is training and a conversation, even if it is with someone in the house who is not all that interested in the parrot. Everyone needs to be on the same page and understand when and how they are reinforcing the parrot.

If you have problem behaviors, it is especially important that everyone in the house understands the plan. Everyone should ignore the screaming parrot and answer only when the parrot says "Hello" if that is your plan for dealing with the behavior. The parrot's relationship with different individuals will vary, and therefore so will the amount of reinforcement the parrot will get from interacting with different persons. However, everyone in the house is still playing a part in teaching the parrot the rules of the house.

As you begin to train tricks, it is okay to have multiple trainers, but only one person should be training any one behavior at a time. If your wife wants to train the parrot to wave and you want to train the parrot to put up his wings, this is fine as long as the parrot has enough attention for all the training sessions. And once the parrot has learned a behavior it is okay for everyone to cue him and reward it. When training, though, it's only one trainer per behavior. This eliminates confusion and makes things a lot less frustrating for the parrot. So let's train some new behaviors!

Evolving with Changes

Training is a conversation you will be having with your parrot for the rest of your lives. Behavior evolves and life changes. You and your parrot will hopefully be navigating these changes for a long time to come. At some point your parrot is going to start doing things you do not like. If you understand the basics of applied behavior analysis and how to train, however, you can easily adjust these behaviors. You will be able to figure out how the parrot is getting reinforced for undesirable behaviors, what to reward instead, and how to live together happily again. Even if you only train your parrot to do a couple of tricks, these tools will keep your relationship strong and pleasant.

Is She Really Going Out With Him?

Ty hated my boyfriend, the handsome Mediterranean (let's call him Mr. Med) who lived with me for six months. The grey parrot hadn't bit me in ten years, but he drew foreign blood for sport. Not that the parrot made much effort to attack. He was more of an opportunistic blood-taster. I told Mr. Med to just leave the parrots alone, to only interact to give them treats, let them build a relationship with him on their own terms, but he wouldn't have it.

Mr. Med felt that since we were both animal trainers, my birds should do as he wished them to do. He was irritated that Ty and the other parrots wouldn't learn the whistles and words he tried to teach them. So he insisted on reaching into their cages to change bowls and papers, chasing parrots that had landed on the floor, and demanding they step up, calling out cues to which the parrots rarely complied and shoving his hand beneath the glaring grey. Ty bit him.

Mr. Med would scream, throw a tantrum, and yell at me to better train my birds. Ty seemed to look at me accusingly as well, but I didn't consider or translate his actions. Instead I worked harder to get things on cue and build confidence.

While I tried to work things out between my beloveds, Mr. Med got busy too. When I wasn't home, he read through my journals and examined what friends wrote in my high school yearbooks, reaching into my private space and then accusing me of not sharing my innermost thoughts. He started fights and would not leave me alone to think and calm down. He made demands and pointed out my flaws. He insisted that I change and when I refused called me selfish. Ty was right. I should have bit him.

It took me almost a year to figure out what Ty saw from the get-go. We all deserve choices and options and positive reinforcement for good behavior. So I listened when Ty fell in love the guy I called the Falconer.

The Falconer messed with the parrot cages only when there was no choice. He never asked the birds to do anything on cue and never expected them to step up for him, although Ty would go anywhere with him. When Ty whistled the Falconer whistled back. They learned to have their own conversations. Ty learned the theme to *"The Good, the Bad and the Ugly,"* apparently their own private song because he has never been willing to whistle it for me. The Falconer gave me space, never made demands, and encouraged the things I loved. Ty was right. He was a good guy.

The Falconer and I didn't make it in the long run. Years later, though, we're close friends and if something happens to me, he'll be inheriting Ty. Unless, of course, someone else wanders into my life, rocks my world, and sweeps Ty off his zygodactyl feet. After all, Ty knows a good thing when he has it.

4

Getting Your Feet Wet:
Simple Training

Much of this chapter consists of basic behaviors that you can build on as you are training more complicated behaviors. These behaviors are broken into small steps, but once your parrot understands them, you can build on them to train many things. As you start, remember that every behavior, even the simple behaviors like stepping up, involve a series of small steps. Training is shaping, and you need to be mindful that your parrot does not know what you are expecting for the end result. Slow, steady, and well planned wins the race.

There are several ways to train any behavior, and in some cases I give you a couple of paths to the same end result. With the more complicated behaviors and with some practice, you may find other ways to train than my suggested path. For now, try it my way and have fun. There is nothing I enjoy more than that moment when a parrot realizes that "good" means a treat and the light bulb goes on. To me it is amazing to see the gears start to move in parrots' minds as they problem-solve and exceed your expectations with their cleverness. Parrots always exceed my expectations, doing surprisingly brilliant things that make me laugh at myself. Surely you will discover that your parrot is clever and amazing too.

Desensitization

It is important that before you present your parrot with anything—a target, a new toy, a prop, or even the clicker—that you make certain he is not afraid of it. Frightening your parrot when you are starting to train will slow things down and undermine your positive relationship. If he has never seen a dollar bill before and you shove it under his beak and startle him, it will take you a much longer time to teach him to take it and carry it. So go slow. Show him anything he hasn't seen before from a distance and see how he reacts. If he cowers or moves away, step back and leave the item somewhere he can see it but where it isn't so close he is uncomfortable. Allow him time to grow accustomed to the item. Then slowly move it closer until you can approach him with it and he is not concerned. Once you are certain your parrot is not afraid of the new item, you can start training with it.

Target Training

If you can train your bird to go to a target and touch it, you can train him to do an amazing amount of things. The uses for leading a parrot with a target are nearly limitless. Targeting can be used to teach a parrot to go into a crate, get a reluctant parrot back into his cage, and turn in circles—and these are just the beginning!

Props Needed: Target

Cue: "Touch" or just the presentation of the target.

Desired Behavior: Parrot walks or flies to target and touches end of target with beak.

Steps:

1. Parrot looks at target.
2. Leans toward target.
3. Touches target.
4. Touches target and releases target.
5. Takes step to get to target to touch it.
6. Continue with holding target farther and farther away for the parrot to come to and touch with his beak.

Instructions

There are many different things that you can use for a target. A wooden drumstick, an empty pen barrel, or anything safe for your parrot to play with will work. I prefer to use chopsticks. They are inexpensive and expendable. I love to use target training as the first thing I train a parrot I have not met before, so I always come to workshops with some chopsticks in my bag of tricks. If I have a parrot that is aggressive or a chewer, I can let him destroy the chopstick and not worry about it. Plastic chopsticks work fine as well. You can use whatever works best for you, however. Keep

There are several ways to train any behavior. As long as you are using positive methods and getting results, the method you use is fine.

You can make targets easily and inexpensively from chopsticks and red food coloring.

in mind that using chopsticks can be helpful if your target has a colored tip. For wooden chopsticks, a bit of nontoxic food coloring on the tip works well and gives the parrot an even more specific target to pinpoint.

Start by showing your parrot the chopstick and making sure he is not afraid of it. A curious parrot is likely to approach the chopstick immediately to investigate. If he does not approach, however, you can reward him for looking at the chopstick and then for getting closer. If the treats are something he enjoys, he will quickly start to try to figure out what it is he is getting rewarded for and begin experimenting. As long as you are consistent, it will become obvious to him that the rewards have something to do with the chopstick.

When your parrot explores the chopstick with his beak, immediately say "good" and reward him. It is possible that he will latch on to the chopstick and not let go for the treat. In that case, just let him have it and play with it. You can get it back when he drops it. Getting to gnaw on the chopstick is a reward in itself. Eventually, though, it won't be as exciting as getting a treat. Usually after playing

Start your target training by showing your parrot the target and making sure he is not afraid of it.

Once your parrot understands that you want him to touch the target and let go, start making him stretch out to reach the target.

with the chopstick a couple of times the parrot will decide he is more interested in getting a treat from you than hanging on to the chopstick.

What you absolutely do not want to do is fight him for it. If you wrestle the target away you could create aggression or just a situation that is not positive in general.

Continue to say "good" when your parrot touches the chopstick until he does this without hesitation and it is obvious that he understands. Then wait for him to touch it and then let go, at which point you mark the event when he lets go. This may happen right away, but the important thing is that he learns that the behavior is to touch and let go. Once he completely understands this, see whether you can get him to stretch his neck out a little to reach the target and then farther. Once he will stretch his body all the way out to touch the stick, see whether you can get him to take a few steps, then a few more—and soon you will be leading him around farther and farther for a treat.

I do not usually use a verbal cue for this behavior, because the presentation of the target works well. However, it is not a bad idea to add a verbal cue, especially if you think you will be training your parrot to target to several different items. You can then generalize the cue to target to various objects. Use a quick short word like "touch" or some other word that comes naturally to you. There is no harm in using both the verbal and the physical cue.

Your Hand as a Target

Training your parrot to a chopstick or some other target is especially helpful because it allows you to extend your reach and move your parrot into some places that might be difficult to reach your hand into. However, you will find when training that your parrot keys into your treat hand as a target. This is not a problem as long as you are mindful of your parrot's attention to your hand. In fact, using your hand as a target can be very helpful when you are training, and you will use this often.

With a closed fist, hold out your treat hand (your right hand if you are right-handed). Hold your hand positioned so that you are ready to give a treat. When your parrot faces your hand positioning his body toward your hand, say "good" and reach over and give him a treat. After you have done this a few times, your parrot will understand that when you present your closed fist, you want him to orient his body toward your hand.

However, you do not want your parrot constantly reaching out to your hand for a treat, so catch him before he leans toward you. Set the criteria for him to be oriented toward your hand but not grabbing for a treat. If you don't mark the event when he leans out but only when he is still and in position, this is the behavior he will offer. He will still lean out when the treat

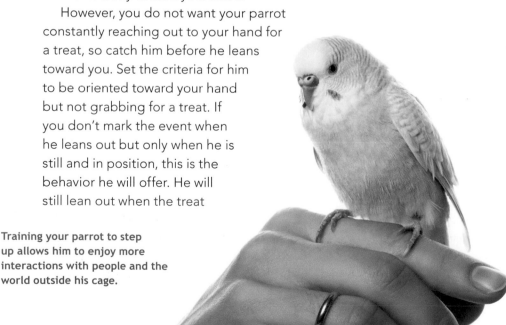

Training your parrot to step up allows him to enjoy more interactions with people and the world outside his cage.

Using Gloves

I have often come across parrot owners who use giant welding gloves when stepping up their parrots in order to avoid being bitten. I see two major problems here. One is that the parrot owner is afraid of her parrot and has not built up a relationship she trusts. The other is that the parrot doesn't trust the owner or he wouldn't bite to begin with. Some parrots are much more fearful of gloves than human hands as well, exacerbating the problem. Then there is the issue that the parrot owner cannot feel the parrot on her hand, which is an important piece of being able to tell whether a parrot is comfortable, nervous, or about to try and fly. It is true that I use gloves when handling birds of prey, but these are gloves a parrot could bite right through; I use them to protect my skin from the needle-sharp talons on my falcon's toes. If your problem is that your parrot's nails are so sharp they are making you bleed, learn how to groom your parrot's nails (as in the next chapter). Don't use a glove as a Band-Aid to fix a problem that could be fixed by training a parrot to step up or have his nails trimmed with positive reinforcement.

appears from your closed fist and is offered to him, but you are trying to avoid having him constantly nipping at your hand for a treat.

Step Up

You will often hear parrot trainers say that stepping up is the most important thing your parrot can learn to do and that he absolutely must step up when you ask. I agree with the important part. A parrot that steps up gets to explore his world a lot more than one who will not get onto your hand. A parrot that steps up has a much larger life and is likely to be well adjusted. Not to that mention he will be enjoyable to be around.

I completely disagree that a parrot "must" step up. A parrot trained through positive reinforcement will step up almost all the time, and that is plenty. So what if there is an emergency? I don't know about you, but if my house is on fire, I'm grabbing my parrots and shoving them into crates or under my shirt on the way out. I'm not asking anyone to step up. I'll happily deal with the repercussions later rather than waste even a second getting my bird out of a dangerous situation. Some behaviorists today feel that the practice of making parrots step up has caused many parrots to be hand-shy and difficult to handle.

The older idea of training a parrot to step involved pushing on his chest with a finger held out until he stepped up to get the pressure off his chest. If your parrot bit you, you ignored it. Basically the parrot had no choice. This is training by using negative reinforcement, or in other words avoidance training. In order to get you to quit pushing or stroking his chest with your finger, he had to step up. This method works, but it does not give the parrot a choice in the matter or anything rewarding once he steps up. Using avoidance training, you may find that it is often difficult to get him to step up and that you are more likely to create a situation that involves aggression. The much better method of training is with positive reinforcement.

Do not press your finger into your bird's chest to make him step up. This can make him afraid of hands.

Props Needed: None required, but you will need a stick or perch if you wish to also train your parrot to step up onto a stick.

Cue: Presentation of hand and, if you wish, a verbal cue of "up"

Desired Behavior: Parrot steps up onto hand when presented.

Steps:

1. Parrot faces your treat hand and your perch hand is positioned for a step-up.
2. Faces treat hand and reaches over perch hand to get treat.
3. Stretches to target treat hand over perch hand.
4. Parrot briefly places one foot on perch hand to target to treat hand.
5. Puts weight on foot on perch hand to target to treat hand.
6. Briefly puts both feet on perch hand to target to treat hand.
7. Puts weight on both feet on perch hand to target treat hand.
8. Puts weight on both feet on perch hand to target treat hand and is comfortable enough to stay.
9. Steps onto perch hand to target treat hand and allows you to move without showing signs of nervousness.

Instructions

Start by orienting your parrot to face you by using your treat hand as a target and your hand held out for him to step up. Your perch hand should be only an inch or so away from your parrot and positioned slightly above his perch. It is easier for parrots to step up than to step down, and you want to make all training as easy and comfortable as you can. Your perch hand can be either held with your palm flat and facing up, with the thumb toward the parrot, or by offering him your pointer finger but keeping it firm and steady so that your parrot has a solid perch to step up onto.

If you want to use a verbal cue, say "up" every time you present your perch hand. Presenting your hand is a physical cue as well, so whether or not you use both is up to you. I have done it both ways; either works fine for me. Wait until you have your parrot's attention. There is no reason to request him to step up if his back is to you, he is playing with a toy, or occupied in some other way. Wait until he is paying attention to you and seems interested in what you are doing. Then cue him.

When he faces you, say "good," and give him a treat. If he seems comfortable with having your perch hand in front of him, get him to target to your closed hand over the perch hand. If he is nervous about this, take your time with him. Don't make him reach too far and move forward in very small steps. You do not want to ask him to step up onto your hand until he is completely comfortable with reaching over your perch hand. When he will take a treat over your perch hand, get him to start to stretch to target, so that he has to position more and more of his body over your perch hand to reach the target.

Once your parrot is confident stretching as far as he can to reach your target hand, cue him and offer your target hand just far enough away that he has to place a foot on your hand to reach the target. He will likely place his foot on your hand long enough to target and get his treat and then immediately pull it back to his perch. That is fine. Let him step back, and keep your

The first step to teaching the step up is for your parrot to lean out from his perch to take a treat.

Once your bird is comfortable reaching for the treat, put your perching hand in position so that he has to reach over it to get a reward.

motions slow and your voice calm. Keep repeating until he is not in a rush to pull his foot off, and get him to reach a bit farther. The next step will be for him to put both feet onto your hand in order to target.

Once he is stepping with both feet confidently and not jumping off your hand right away you can start to move a bit while he perches on your hand. Staying on your hand after stepping up is another behavior. So only expect him to stay on for a few moments and reward him for staying as well as stepping up. If at any time he reaches a foot behind himself or leans as if he wants to be off your hand, let him go back to his perch. Then wait for him to look interested in stepping up and try again. As you begin to walk around with him, give him a treat for sitting calmly every 5 seconds or so, then every 10 seconds, and then every 20 seconds. Soon you won't have to reward him for staying except for maybe a cuddle or transporting him to a fun place to play or hang out.

If Your Parrot Is Hand-Shy

Some parrots come from a situation where they have been forced to step up and are afraid of hands. Before you try to train your parrot to step up, make sure he is

How to Present Treats

When you are rewarding a parrot with treats it is important to keep them handy but hidden. You also must give out only one piece at a time. If you have never done this before, figuring out how to hold your treats might be a little perplexing.

Place treats broken into small pieces in the palm of your hand and close your fingers over them with your thumb on the outside, hiding the treats inside. You can then use your thumb to move treats up between your thumb and index finger to present to your parrot for a reward. This way all the treats except for what you are handing your parrot stay hidden. Your parrot will not see what the reward is going to be. He will also not be able to grab a big mouthful when you hand him a treat; he will only get what your hand him. Sometimes when I end a training session and want to give the parrot a jackpot, I will open up my fingers and let him grab several beakfuls of whatever he wants the most in my hand.

When your parrot is reliably reaching for the treat, start rewarding him only when he puts one foot on your hand.

confident being near your hands. If you present a hand to step up onto and your parrot moves away and does not want to come near, you have some additional training to do. Bird trainer Barbara Heidenreich has developed a wonderful technique for parrots that are afraid to come near hands, and I suggest this as a starting point.

Set up a sturdy perch for your parrot to get onto in his cage or perhaps bolted to the outside of the cage. Make sure that it is one he can get to that leaves room for you to get your hand positioned at the end of the perch without crowding your parrot. Target your parrot to the perch with your treat hand. Then place your perch hand at the end of the perch, creating a sturdy extension of its surface. Now in small steps get your parrot closer and closer to the hand at the end of the perch, targeting him to your treat hand. Once he is comfortable getting close, get him to place a foot onto your hand. Follow this with having him placing both feet onto your hand. Do repetitions until your parrot does not hesitate and is very comfortable on your perch hand. This may take some time with a hand-shy bird, but once he will sidle right off the side of the perch and onto your hand, he should be far more comfortable with hands. Then you can train him to step up.

My Parrot Already Knows How to Step Up

If your parrot already knows how to step up, you obviously do not need to start at the very beginning steps and train from start to finish. However, you should definitely give some thought to how and when you ask your parrot to step up. The most important thing is that you ask. Give your parrot the opportunity to decide whether or not to step up.

If you reward your parrot with a treat, a toy he likes, or some quality time with you when he steps up, he will be more likely to step up. If he doesn't step up, shut the cage door and go about your business. He doesn't get rewarded, and that is something that he will definitely consider if he was rewarded in the past. Next time you ask, he will probably come with you right away. A parrot that has a history of getting more reinforcement for stepping up than for staying in the cage will almost always step up for you.

A Parrot on Your Shoulder

The image of a parrot sitting on a pirate's shoulder is an iconic one. In fact parrots are frequently depicted and photographed sitting on their owners' shoulders. You have probably heard at least once that this is a bad idea. Maybe you've heard that parrots become dominant when they sit on your shoulder or that you might lose an eye. Neither of these things is true. However, a parrot on your shoulder can be troublesome. I rarely let parrots on my shoulder, because I cannot see their body language well and figure out what they might be going to do next. I cannot see aggression building and find them much more difficult to manage. So my preference is to keep parrots on my hand, on the back of my chair, or in their play area when I have them out of their cages. If you do not find you have problems with your parrot on your shoulder, by all means let him perch there. If you start having issues, however, it is time to keep your parrot in more manageable places.

Be careful not to train latency. If you stand there offering your hand over and over he will come when he feels like it. He will be slow about it because he knows he has all the time in the world to get his treat. You should also avoid showing him bigger and bigger treats until he decides to step up. If you do this he will learn that if he waits before stepping up, he will get something much better for a reward. Show your hand, but give him only a couple of chances to step up. If he does, give him a treat or a toy or a cuddle and make it a wonderful surprise.

Stick Training

Training your parrot to step up onto a wooden perch can be very helpful. If your hand is injured or someone who is nervous about having parrots on their hand has to care for your parrots while you are ill or away, being able to use a stick will make things easier. Also, if you find that you are battling an aggression issue between the parrot and another member of

A method for training a hand-shy bird is to start by placing your hand at the end of the perch and having him sidestep onto your hand to get the treat.

Give your parrot only a few chances to step up. He will learn that stepping up on cue is the way to earn a reward.

the household, the stick can be a way to manage the parrot while you work through the aggressive behavior.

Find a sturdy perch that is an appropriate width for your parrot's feet. Make sure that it is not too slippery and is overall comfortable. Test to see whether your parrot is comfortable around it. You may have to desensitize him to the perch before you train. Then follow all the directions to training step up using the stick instead of your hand as a perch.

It is often trickier to train a parrot to step down into his cage than it is to train him to step up.

Step Down

Of course, stepping up is great, but you also need your parrot to step down. Even if you have a parrot that has absolutely no issue with stepping up, you may have a much bigger problem with stepping down. Parrots that are confident and comfortable with their caregivers often would prefer hanging out with their human to being anywhere else. So getting down or going back into the cage is often nowhere nearly as reinforcing as being attached to their person. It is wonderful to have a parrot that is that into you, but there are times when you really need to put your parrot onto a perch or into his cage. You can easily train this. The only real trick is the reinforcement.

Props Needed: None. You will use your hand as a target.

Cue: You can use a physical cue such as directing your parrot with the index finger of your treat hand and/or use a verbal cue like "Off" or "Down".

Desired Behavior: Parrot steps off onto perch.

Steps:

1. Parrot is positioned in front of desired perch and looks at it.
2. Parrot is positioned in front of perch and orients toward closed target hand.
3. Reaches over perch for target.
4. Places one foot on perch while reaching for target.
5. Places both feet on perch while reaching for target.

Directions

If your parrot has learned to step up, this training should go very quickly. Position your parrot in front of the perch and make sure he does not lean away or act fearful. If he does, get him as close as you can without him reacting and reward him for sitting calmly in front of the perch. Next you can get him closer and closer in approximations and with rewards until he can be positioned to step up and sit calmly.

Hold your parrot slightly below the perch you want him to step onto and an inch or so away. Then hold your target hand so that he has to reach over the perch. Once he is reaching over, get him to set up with one foot and then with both. Don't forget to cue, mark the event, and reward at each step. This should go very quickly and he may even just step right off the first time if he is comfortable with the perch. What you should be mindful of are the rewards.

If you are consistently having trouble with a sticky-footed parrot that is determined not to leave your hand, remember that a behavior repeats itself only if it is reinforced. Is your parrot getting enough reinforcement for stepping off?

It's a good idea to train your parrot to step down to other people.

This can be particularly challenging if you are having him step off into his cage where he is often locked up when playtime outside is over. You can make it more reinforcing by placing new toys and favorite treats inside.

Another way to get a parrot to step down more consistently is to make sure that you do frequent repetitions. If the only reason your parrot is stepped down into his cage is because you are leaving him for the rest of the day or night, nothing may be reinforcing enough in the cage. Instead, make an effort to occasionally step him off into the cage for a treat and then step him right back up. Once in a while step him off and just leave him for a few minutes and then pick him back up. If he is never sure how long he will be staying, he has no reason to think that being with you is more reinforcing. Whenever a behavior breaks down, always go back to considering the consequence of the behavior and whether it is reinforcing or not.

Stepping Down to Other People

If you like to take your parrot places or have frequent guests, you may want your parrot to be comfortable stepping off you and up for other people. The more positive experiences your parrot has with strangers, the more likely he will be eager to step up for people he has never met. It is up to you to make sure he gets such experience and that it remains positive.

Whatever you do, don't step your parrot up onto someone who is afraid of parrots just to prove your bird is wonderful or to tease the person who is afraid. This is not fair to your friend or to your parrot. Both of them are likely to have a bad experience and then not want to try again. Whoever handles your parrot should have a steady hand, want to give holding your parrot a try, and understand how the step-up is going to work.

Start by having the new person offer the parrot a treat. This helps make sure your parrot is not nervous and that his first experience with the stranger is a positive one. Next, hold your parrot near your friend and reward him for sitting calmly on your hand. If he is obviously comfortable being near your friend, have your friend hold out her arm nice and steady. Then use your treat hand to target your parrot to step off your hand and onto your friend's arm with the same approximations described for stepping off. Just treat your friend's arm like another perch and cue, mark the behavior, and reward it. Just be sure to watch both your parrot and your friend to make sure they are both comfortable at all times.

Once your parrot is confident and stepping onto your friend's arm without hesitation, you can have your friend take over the targeting and reinforcing. Once she is comfortable and confident with cuing and reinforcing the behavior, you can put your parrot on a perch and have your friend step him up as described in the section on training the step up. This stage should go quickly. In fact, your parrot might just step right up with no hesitation without going through the training steps.

Stationing

Another simple behavior to train that is incredibly helpful is stationing. Teaching an animal to station means training him to go to a designated spot and stay there. This behavior can be very helpful in combating problem behaviors. There are many things that a parrot cannot do while stationing at the same time. A parrot cannot be on the floor chasing after feet and climbing to the top of his cage to station for a treat at the same time. A parrot cannot be roaming the house looking for attention and stationing on his playstand at the same time. At bird shows with flighted parrots, we trained them to station on their perches to wait for a treat and to be picked up. That way our parrots can't try to rush out the door while we are trying to collect them for the show. I have trained aggressive raptors to station at the back of their cages for rewards when it was time to clean out cages and change bath pans. There are many situations in which stationing can be very helpful.

Teaching your parrot to station can help manage behavior problems and help keep your parrot safe.

Props Needed: A location to station, perhaps marked with a red dot. Some examples are a playstand or the top of your parrot's cage.

Cue: Use your index finger to point to the station and also a verbal cue like "Station".

Desired Behavior: Parrot goes to his station and waits.

Steps:

1. Parrot orients toward the station.
2. Moves toward the station.
3. Steps on station.
4. Takes a step to get to station.
5. Takes several steps to get to station.
6. Stays on station for 5 seconds.
7. Stays on station for 10 seconds.
8. Stays on station for 15 seconds and so on.

Directions

First choose where you would like your parrot to go. If you are just stationing him in his cage, choose a particular perch and stick to rewarding for going to only that perch when cued to station. If you have a place you want him to go to outside the cage, you should make sure it is obvious where exactly you want your parrot to go. If his station is on a playstand, mark the perch you want him on with a nontoxic red

Training a Geriatric Parrot

Yes, you can train an old parrot new tricks! Sometimes you have to make allowances for old age. A parrot that has arthritis or has difficulties getting around because of his age may need some help. If he has trouble balancing on perches because he does not grip well anymore, wrap the perch you are training with in vet wrap (a type of elastic bandage) or outdoor carpeting that will make it easier to grip. Just make sure you do not use anything your parrot could get his toes caught on. If he has trouble balancing because he has wing issues, train him in places where he will not fall, like a very short perch on a table. If you have an older parrot you should do everything you can to keep him comfortable and set him up for success.

dot. This will make training more clear and precise.

Place your parrot near the perch or the mark you want him to station on. Cue him and, using a target, orient his body toward the station. When he is facing the station, mark the event with "good" and reward him. Next, see whether you can get him to move toward the station. Cue, mark, reward. Then see whether you can get him onto the perch by targeting and rewarding him. Next, get him to stand exactly on the spot where the station is marked.

Once your parrot has been rewarded for standing on the station spot, he will likely wander off it. Cue him, target him to the exact spot, and then mark the event and reward him. Soon he will understand that stationing means standing on the marked spot. Once your parrot understands this, pick him up, set him down just slightly farther away than he was last time, and cue him to station. Move him farther and farther away—still targeting to the station—until he will go to the station from several feet away.

Once you train your parrot to go to his station, start training him to stay there for longer and longer periods of time.

Make sure staying on his station is a positive experience for your parrot.

Once he is doing this readily and without hesitation, try phasing out the target. See if you can get him to the spot with minimal use of the target, presenting it only if he stops or gets distracted. Continue repetitions using the target less and less until he goes straight to the station without needing the direction of the target. You should be able to phase out the target fairly quickly, using a quick point to the station instead.

Once you have trained your parrot to go to the station, you can then train him to stay on the station. Those are two separate behaviors that you will chain together. Always focus on one behavior at a time so as not to confuse your parrot. So make sure he understands the cue to go to the station, and then you can focus on getting him to stay on the station. Start by quickly rewarding after he has stationed. Wait for him to finish his reward for going there; then, before he starts thinking about stepping off, say "good" and give him a treat. At first you will only be rewarding him for staying on the station for a few seconds, but slowly draw it out, trying to get him to stay longer and longer.

If your parrot steps off the station and wanders when you are trying to train him to stay, wait a few moments and then cue him to go to the station. Reward him and then start again rewarding him for waiting. Soon you should be able to get your parrot to sit for some time. Once this behavior is trained, be sure to reinforce your parrot for staying on the station at different intervals. For example, reward him for staying just a few seconds and other times for staying 20 seconds. If your parrot has learned to stay for long periods of time, you will still have to reinforce the behavior to keep it repeating.

Stationing can be particularly helpful if you have a parrot that nips when you are changing out his bowls. Additionally, it is a very simple behavior to maintain. If you don't take bowls out—or even more importantly don't put bowls full of delicious food back into the cage unless your parrot is sitting at his station—he will soon learn to go there and stay. In fact, you might find that when your parrot wants a bowl full of treats he will station himself hoping you will notice and reward him. And if you appreciate this behavior, it wouldn't hurt to do just that!

Conclusion

Targeting, stepping up, stepping down, and stationing are all fairly easy behaviors to train and a great way get your feet wet with training. They are also behaviors that will be valuable in everything else you train, whether you are training for tricks or for day-to-day living. So if you have just successfully trained your bird to target, congratulations! Let's put your new skills to work on some things that will make life easier for you and your parrot.

Where You Are Sitting

Ty has a rope swing, a concrete perch, a comfy piece of cholla cactus skeleton, and a manzanita wood perch at the top of the cage, with a grand view of his immediate world. He also knows that if he asks, I'll take him to perch in the bathroom where he can pace on top of the shower doors and let his voice echo in the admirable acoustics. The world is his oyster as far as sitting arrangements in a person's home go. None of these places, however, are his favorite perch. His favorite perch is too small to support him, uncomfortably thin beneath his feet, and has the least attractive view of all his choices. Still, I understand.

I get it. I'm happy to perch just about anywhere. Although I feel like a rock star when I'm sitting on Italian leather and half my age when I'm nestled in a bean bag, it's more than that. I'm blissful sitting at the edge of a cliff, looking over the ocean. I also love to swing in a tire, even if it's dirty and smells like rubber. It's about more than the place you're sitting.

It's a hike to Ty's favorite perch. It takes some work.

Ty climbs out of his cage and up the side of it where his food dishes are safely locked in. Small doors open from the outside so that the bowls can be removed but not pushed out. Ty knows these doors well. They aren't particularly difficult to open. A beak can lift and slide them without too much effort, but it takes a little maneuvering. The real challenge is pushing the door open just far enough that a heavy-breasted parrot can climb on top of the door without having it swing flush against the cage. This takes some strategy. Then once he has managed to get atop this makeshift perch, adjustments are required for perfect alignment. It's a joy to watch, really, parrot brain and body focused and working in tandem. The whole process takes several minutes, and the end result is surely an uncomfortable sit—but it's where Ty loves to be.

I watched him one morning as he ignored the myriad toys in his cage, more concerned about his station. I admired his tinkering, adjusting, and his obvious contentment with his final position. So when his work was done I got up to do mine, scratching him on the head as I passed. It was Sunday, but Ty was right. The best places, the most satisfying places to sit are the ones that you worked to get to and had work to do to get there.

Parrots, like all other animals (and people too) enjoy the stimulation of challenges and interacting with their world. Training is one way to provide these things, and it enhances their lives. So keep training!

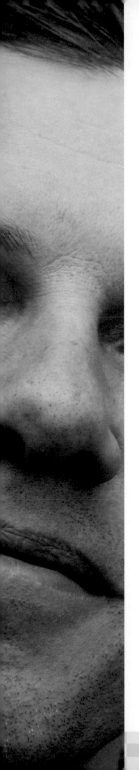

5

Training for Better Living

Even if you are not sure that you want to train your parrot to do a bunch of tricks, there are numerous things you can spend your time training that are helpful in day-to-day living. Many of the behaviors this chapter discusses are rarely trained. Instead, the parrot is forced to simply tolerate conditions that could have been improved for him by training him to not only accept them but also even find them rewarding in some fashion. This is a shame because it is easy to make the world a much better place for your parrot through training.

Imagine if someone held you down to clip your nails, dunked you under the showerhead every morning, and pushed you into your car to get to work. Even if they were nice about it and you were happy to be clean and groomed, you would probably feel as though you didn't have a lot of control in your life. It might even make you less likely to interact with your environment and less curious about your world.

This is a good description of depression and not an unusual description of how many animals that have no control over their environment act. Give your parrot back the reins to his life!

Start training your parrot to bathe by placing him near the running faucet.

Training to Bathe

The most common way people train a parrot to bathe is by simply squirting the bird or putting him under a spray of water. Reasoning that a parrot has to bathe for proper feather care and that the water is not hurting him, people feel this is better than letting him choose not to bathe at all. This is unfortunate because a parrot trained this way may or may not learn to enjoy bathing.

If your parrot is very young and has never had a bath, you should give him the opportunity to discover the bathwater on his own. Bathing is often reinforcing in itself to parrots—some individuals really enjoy bathing, while others do not—but the parrot should discover that bathing is fun without any pressure from you. First try training your parrot to bathe by reinforcing himself.

Props Needed: Running faucet in kitchen sink

Cue: Running water

Desired Behavior: Parrot gets in and out of water, bathing

Steps:

1. Parrot looks at water.
2. Approaches water.
3. Puts beak into water.
4. Gets into and out of water.

Instructions

Training to bathe is the simplest training of all. You simply have to be there to facilitate and make sure that nothing happens to frighten your parrot. An easy way to do this is to turn on the kitchen sink. Our parrots often see us doing dishes in the sink and will be familiar with the area and the running water. Turn on the faucet and walk your parrot over, checking that he is not nervous. Place your parrot on the counter near the water. Make sure the counter is not too slippery; if it is, put down a towel so he does not slip. If you have a double sink, you may want to place a towel over the divider between the two sinks to give your parrot some traction if he wants to walk across the divider and get under the running faucet. You can play in the water yourself if you like, splashing and making encouraging noises, enticing him to come over. Just set him up so that he can wander over, stick his beak into the water, and walk away if he is unsure. Likely he will come right back to the water and quickly discover that getting into it is a fun time. Once he is a fan of the bath, you can bring him over and let him bathe whenever you think he might want a bath; just don't ever force him.

You can train a parrot with operant conditioning to take a bath by allowing

Most parrots will take a drink from the faucet without any prompting. With only a little guidance, they will happily enter the water.

him to reinforce himself, or, if you have a reluctant parrot, you can be the giver of reinforcement and shape the behavior. You use the same steps as above except that you direct the bathing.

Leave the water running in the sink and step your parrot onto the counter. (You may have to do some repetitions on and off the counter if your parrot is uncomfortable with standing on it.) Once your parrot is comfortable standing on the counter, train him to bathe by rewarding each step progressively. To get him closer and closer to the water, use your hand as a target and reward him first for looking at the water, then for moving toward it, then for putting his beak into it, and eventually for getting all the way in.

At any time he is uncomfortable he can back out or quit altogether, and you can pick up your training session again later. And once you get him going to the water on his own you can ask him to step up and position him with your hand so that he can move all the way into the water for rewards. Pretty soon you will have a parrot that has learned that bathing is fun and enjoyable and that getting into the water will likely be its own reward.

Sure, a lot of us have learned how to swim by being thrown into the water, but who wants to learn that way when you can just as easily put on your floaties and slowly test the water on your own? Life should be a self-explored adventure, not a task that is forced on us. Those of us who have found our way by exploring and being in control are well adjusted and on the lookout for fun. This is similar for all animals. So give your parrot a chance to delight in the simple things in life, like taking a bath!

Training for Nail Trimming

Some parrots never need to have their nails trimmed. If they have a nice variety of perches, including a concrete perch, their nails often will stay blunt. You can

You can train your parrot to use a shower perch by employing similar steps as when training him to bathe in the sink.

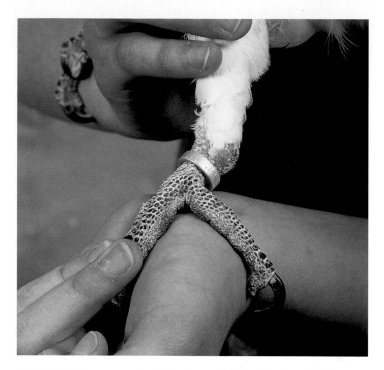

It's helpful if your parrot is already used to you handling his feet before training the nail trim.

facilitate blunt nails just by paying attention to which ones are your parrot's favorite perches. Usually the favorite perch in a parrot's cage is the one that is highest. When your parrot's nails start to get sharp, switch out the favorite perch for a concrete one to wear down his nails. Sometimes concrete perches can be rough on the bottoms of a parrot's feet, so check his feet regularly. If they look irritated, change the perches back the way they were or replace the rough one. This is easier than even training a parrot to allow you to trim his nails, but training a nail trim is not too hard.

Props Needed: Nail clippers

Cue: Presentation of the nail clippers with hand signal.

Desired Behavior: Parrot presents toes for clipping.

Steps:

1. Parrot looks at clippers.
2. Moves near clippers.
3. Moves right next to clippers.
4. Lifts foot.
5. Sets foot on hand next to clippers.
6. Keeps foot on hand, leaving other foot on perch.
7. Allows toe to be touched with clippers.
8. Keeps foot on hand while toes are manipulated.
9. Allows clippers to be opened and shut near toenail.
10. Allows nail to be clipped.

Instructions

To start, make sure you have and use nail clippers that are meant for parrots. If the nail is cut into the quick or crushed, you could have bleeding, which is dangerous to the parrot. Also, if the clip is painful your parrot will associate the clippers with a negative experience and you'll find you have a long haul ahead in training the behavior.

Being Mindful of Your Motions

When you are training, it's important to pay attention not only to your parrot's body language but also to your own motions. It is easy to forget what you are doing with your arms and hands when you are focused on getting your parrot to pay attention and complete the next step in his training. I often see beginning trainers distracting their parrots—sometimes even making them nervous—with their quick motions and their positioning over the bird. Keep your hand motions smooth and slow. Move carefully and slowly. Do not dart about, and don't stomp in frustration when your parrot does not understand what you are asking. Stay calm as well when he does have a breakthrough. Also try not loom over your bird or crowd him, making him feel cornered or uncomfortable. If you are mindful of your own motions and how your parrot is reacting to you, this can help speed up the process of training and make it less frustrating.

If your parrot is afraid of the clippers, take the time to desensitize him to them before training the nail trim.

Make sure your parrot isn't frightened by the clippers; if he is, take the time to desensitize him. Once he is desensitized and you pair the clippers with training and rewards, you'll find that he becomes pleasantly excited rather than fearful to see the clippers. Once you are certain that the clippers are not a source of concern to your bird, reward him for being close to them. Use your target hand to orient him in the direction of the clippers and reward him for this as well. With your event marker and your reinforcement, help him to understand that the clippers are part of the training.

Your next step is to train him to get his foot in a position that allows you to clip the nails. Hold the clippers in your left hand so that they are peeking out and next to where your parrot will put his foot. Since your parrot has been trained to step up and will offer a foot when you hold out your hand, use this to your advantage. Offer your hand, but as soon as he lifts his food mark the event and reward him. You just want him to lift his foot. If you are not fast enough and he steps up, that is okay. Use your target hand to get him back on the perch, reward him, and try again.

Try to position your hand in such a way that your parrot is encouraged to lift a foot as if to step up but will have some difficulty doing anything but placing one foot onto your hand. Hold your hand a bit higher than you normally would for a step-up. Make sure that he can see the clippers peeking out as well. Reward him for placing his foot on your hand and gradually get him to keep his foot there longer and longer.

During this training, you will be reinforcing rapidly and often and your timing will be important. You want just one foot on the hand and staying there. Your parrot will likely not want to leave the foot on your hand for more than a half of a second. So you will have to keep giving him rewards. Either foot is fine because you will need to trim both. And once your parrot understands that you are cuing him for a nail trimming, he will know to give you just one foot and give you the one that is closest to your left hand.

Once your parrot is leaving his foot on your hand for a few seconds, you can start touching his toes and then rewarding him. When he allows this without discomfort or fear, start manipulating his toes as you would if you were going

Domestic vs. Wild

Try to keep in mind that training a parrot is not like training a dog. We have spent thousands of years breeding dogs for traits that include the desire to please and behavior that we appreciate. Your parrot is just a couple of generations removed from the wild. That means that he still functions like a wild animal. He reacts to his environment in ways that would serve him in the wilderness, and unless something is in it for him, he does not care whether or not you appreciate his behavior. Dogs, on the other hand, are concerned about our reactions to them, paying attention to our tone of voice and actions that demonstrate we are displeased. So dogs will often figure out what is and is not acceptable behavior from our subtle reactions. In contrast, parrots do not have this ability. Parrots require much clearer communication.

to trim the nails and reward him. Next, take the clippers in your treat hand and open and close them. Let them go, leaving them in your perch hand, and reward the parrot. At this point he should be holding his foot on your hand for several seconds and you should be able to wait that long to reinforce him.

Once you are able to open and close the clippers with enough time to clip a nail, start positioning the clippers on his nails and reward him. Don't clip yet; wait until he is holding his toes in position long enough that you have plenty of time to clip a nail and a few seconds to spare. Once he is there, clip and reward.

Remember that if he does not leave his foot in position, do not hold it. Let him pull it back and start again. This training can take several sessions, and if you are

After training this behavior, your parrot will present his foot and hold it still for the nail trim on cue.

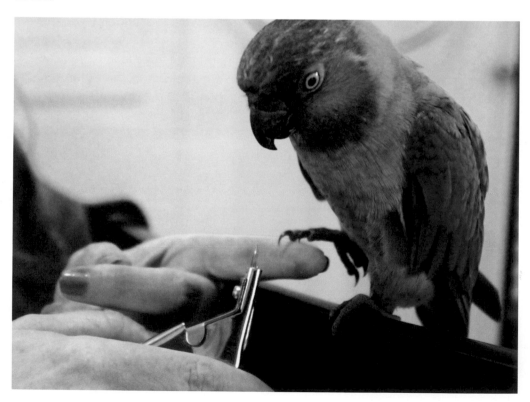

Too Much and Too Little Motivation

You want to end the training session or change treats if your bird loses interest. If you find your bird frequently has no motivation to participate in training, it is obvious that you need to strategize. Perhaps you should get your parrot a checkup at the veterinarian to see whether there is some underlying problem. What about a bird that is overly motivated? This is also something you should pay attention to and address. A bird that is overly motivated may not be getting enough to eat. He may also have medical issues and should see a vet. Your parrot should be happy to get a treat, but not completely uninterested or ravenous.

only training once or twice a day (which is perfectly fine) it may take you several days as well. Be patient and enjoy the progress that you are making.

You may find that your biggest problem is that the parrot wants to play with the clippers (even if he was scared of them only a few days before). Do not fight your bird for the clippers. Just like training with chopsticks, let him take them, play with them, and drop them. You can get his attention with your target hand and get him back to the session. If he is completely enamored with the clippers and has no interest in the treats, chances are your training session is ending. Try to get one more repetition of the step you are on and then end the session.

If you are worried about this being a little complicated to train, you may want to skip to the next chapter and try training the wave first; the wave has similar steps but does not involve props. Once you train a wave both you and your bird will have some experience in learning a behavior that starts similar to a step-up, and you both may have an easier time with training the nail trim.

The Hanging Nail Trim

An alternative way of training a nail trim is to reward your parrot for hanging from the inside of a cage while you are on the outside. If you can set this up, it eliminates your parrot's having a chance to play with the clippers and also eliminates any confusion about stepping onto your hand. The downside is that you have trained your parrot to hang on the side of his cage, and this may not be desirable. If you choose to try to train by this method you will skip the step of having the parrot lift his foot and place it on your hand, but all the rest of the steps are the same. Use slow approximations to get your parrot to allow you to touch his toes, and then manipulate his toes, bring the clippers near, open and shut them near his toes, and eventually clip his nails.

Towel Training

Any time a parrot needs treatment or an examination at the veterinarian, chances are that he should be wrapped in a towel. Often it happens that birds that have been grabbed up in a towel without being trained are terrified of towels and just seeing one frightens them. This is unfortunate because it means that a sick parrot that is already stressed may be further stressed by being wrapped in a towel.

If your parrot has never had any experience with a towel,

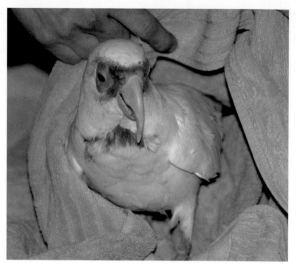

Training your parrot to accept—even enjoy—being wrapped in a towel can make veterinary visits much less stressful for him.

Once your parrot is comfortable with the towel, slowly train him to allow you to pull it over him.

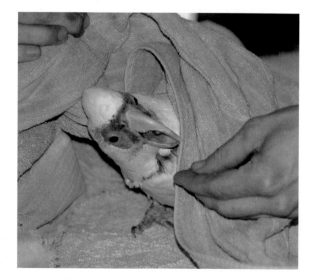

then training him to let you bundle him up is a piece of cake. You do not have to make it a proper training session, you simply need to introduce the towel while keeping it positive and making it fun. Play is the reinforcement that rewards the behavior of interacting with the towel.

Be mindful of your parrot's initial reaction to the towel. If he is afraid of it, leave the towel lying harmlessly on the floor. Give him a chance to desensitize and then make play time happen on the towel. As long as you watch to make sure you are not scaring your parrot,

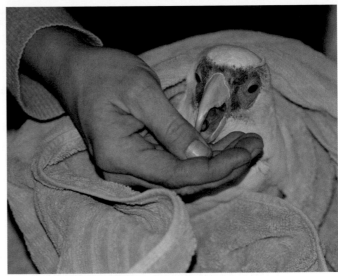

When training toweling, reward your parrot frequently so he has positive associations with the towel.

you can play hide-and-seek with the towel, peek-a-boo, and even wrap him up in it to play. Just go slowly and always stop if he seems nervous. Pretty soon you will have a parrot who is ready to play whenever he sees a towel. Then even if he is occasionally wrapped up for something that is a bit negative, like a vet exam, he will have so much positive history with the towel that he won't necessarily associate the negative experience with it.

If you have a parrot that is terrified of towels, however, you can methodically train him to trust and even enjoy towels. It will take some time and patience, but it could be worth it in the long run to save your bird from experiencing stress when he needs to be restrained. Start by desensitizing him, leaving the towel somewhere he can see it, and slowly getting it closer. This could take anywhere from a matter of minutes to weeks depending on how your parrot reacts to the towel. If he is nervous of the towel, take your time with the desensitization process. Leave the towel on the floor, then hang it from places level with your parrot while slowly getting closer. Move about with the towel and reward your parrot for letting you get close with it. When he is comfortable with the towel being moved near and around him, place the towel on a table where you can start to train with him.

Props Needed: Towel

Cue: Presentation of the towel.

Desired Behavior: Parrot climbs onto towel and allows being wrapped in it.

Steps:

1. Parrot looks at the towel while exhibiting calm behavior.
2. Parrot orients toward the towel.
3. Steps on the towel.
4. Steps on the towel and stays.
5. Stays on the towel while a corner is moved.
6. Stays on the towel while a corner is positioned over the parrot.
7. Allows towel to be draped on body.
8. Allows towel to be draped on both sides of body.
9. Is entirely wrapped in towel.

Instructions

Set your parrot near the towel and reward him. Reward him again when he looks at towel. Using your target hand, orient him toward the towel and reward him.

Handicapped Parrots

If you have a parrot that is handicapped—he could be missing a foot, missing part of a wing, or blind, for example—you can still train him. In fact, it may be crucial that you do train him. All animals want to be able to interact with their environment. Many parrots with handicaps figure out work-arounds all on their own, but you can help by training your disabled parrot. A blind parrot might be trained to target with sound. Perhaps you could train him to come to a spot where you are tapping your finger to lead the way. A parrot that is missing a foot or part of wing may have his environment adjusted to allow him greater mobility, with a subsequent training to behaviors that are within his ability to perform. Even training small things keep a bird's brain busy and help a parrot enjoy his world.

Now take him one step closer at a time until he will step onto the towel without hesitation. If you have desensitized him, this may happen very quickly. Your bigger challenge is going to be getting him to allow the towel to touch him, so take it very slowly. If any next step makes him uncomfortable, let him jump off the towel and then target him back to it and reward him.

Once he will step onto the towel, use rewards to get him to stay on it for longer and longer periods of time. Your goal is for your parrot to stay on the towel long enough that you can wrap a towel around him. Then slowly start by taking the corner of the towel and moving it, rewarding your parrot when he stays. Work on touching him with the towel and then draping it over him one side at a time. Ultimately you will be able to wrap the towel all the way around him.

When your parrot is confident from his training, be sure to change the color of towels and, if he is nervous, repeat these steps. This way he will learn to generalize and not fear any towels. Once your training is complete, be sure to incorporate the towel into play time. If you consistently keep it positive and allow him to become comfortable at his own pace, he will eventually look at the towel as a source of fun.

At first, you will be rewarding your parrot for looking at the crate and then for just going near it.

Using a target is helpful for carrier training so that you do not have to reach in with your hand to lead the parrot inside.

Carrier Training

You will find it extremely convenient if your parrot happily enters his carrier, instead of being afraid of it and putting up a fight. Even if you do not take your parrot on trips very often, there will be times when you have to put him into a carrier and move him. These times include trips to the vet, boarding him while you are on vacation, moving to a new home, and during emergencies, such as floods, wildfires, or hurricanes. It is not difficult to train a parrot to go into his carrier. Having a parrot that is happy to jump in will save you a lot of headaches and eliminate some stress from your parrot's life.

If you leave an open crate in your parrot's play area with toys in it and give him opportunities to play, explore, and discover treats inside the crate, you will have a much easier time training your parrot to get into a crate on cue and be comfortable riding in it. He will already have had positive experiences and will go right in to look for good stuff. Then you can work on training him to be comfortable while staying inside and being moved. However, if your parrot has had unpleasant experiences with a crate, you will have to start from scratch.

Props Needed: Crate and target.

Cue: Physical cue of pointing to the crate and verbal cue of saying "Load" or "Crate".

Desired Behavior: Parrot walks into the crate and allows door to be shut behind him.

Steps:

1. Parrot looks at crate.
2. Orients toward crate.
3. Moves toward crate.
4. Stands in front of crate.
5. Puts head into crate.
6. Puts one foot onto crate.
7. Steps with both feet onto crate.
8. Takes a step inside crate.
9. Walks part way into the crate.
10. Steps up onto the perch in the crate.
11. Walks in to perch and allows door to be closed and then opened.
12. Allows door to be closed for several seconds.
13. Stays in crate comfortably for several minutes.

Instructions

Start by making sure that the carrier is comfortable for your parrot. The perch

Carrier Training Tip

When you place your pet carrier in your vehicle with your parrot, be sure to line the perch up with the motion of the vehicle. Think about what it is like standing on a bus. It is much easier to balance during stops and starts if you can lean sideways into the movement of the vehicle. If your parrot is facing in the direction of the movement he will get thrown forward and backward, making for a less than enjoyable ride.

should be at a level that is easy to step up onto and positioned so that you can shut the door and your parrot can turn around without smashing his tail. The carrier should be big enough for your bird to turn around. If the door on the crate is going to be in the way or it will shut on its own, it is a good idea to remove it for the initial training and put it back on when your parrot is going inside and staying on the perch.

Set your parrot near the carrier, reward him, and reward him for looking at the carrier and orienting himself toward it. Target him closer, cuing and rewarding small steps if he is nervous. If he has no issues with the crate, you can target him right up to it. Get him to touch a target at the edge of the carrier and reward him. Then work on getting one foot and then both feet onto the lip of the carrier.

Using a target is helpful in training this behavior so that do not have to reach in with your parrot to target him. Instead you can slip your target through the side bars of the carrier, asking him to target a little farther inside each time until you can get him to walk in and station on the perch inside. When you reward him, you can drop treats inside. Try not to drop treats inside to lead him in. This may slow down the training because your parrot can then look inside and decide whether or not the reward is worth walking inside for. Leave him guessing what he is getting and give him the treats after you mark the event rather than baiting him into the crate.

Once he is comfortably sitting on the perch and will stay there for several seconds, reward him for staying, shut the door for a moment without latching it, and reward him for sitting with the door shut. If you shut the door and he tries to bolt, open the door and let him out. You do not want to trap him inside if he is that nervous; it will undermine your training session. If he

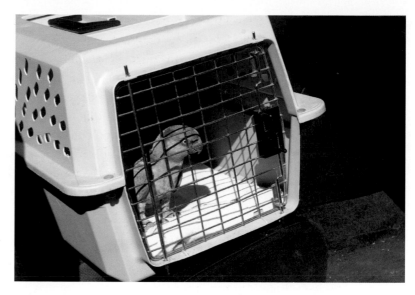

When your parrot is comfortable in his crate while you carry it, you are ready to begin training him to ride in the car.

sits with confidence and lets you shut the door to the crate, you can ask him to sit for longer and longer intervals until you shut the door and latch it.

After your parrot understands what he is being asked to do when you point to the carrier and say "Load", you can phase out the target. Once he understands he is being rewarded for going to the perch and staying, he will no longer need the prompt of the target. You will be able to ask him to "Load", shut the door behind him, and then give him a treat or a toy. A toy he enjoys will work well, because it will give him something to do for a while inside the carrier.

Once you have him loading into the carrier on cue, take the time to also get him comfortable with being moved. Pick up the carrier carefully. Do not swing it. Keep it steady and make the ride smooth when you walk him around, giving him a reward, approximating steps as you have done with all the other behaviors until he could comfortably go for a ride in the carrier. Once you get to the point where you are ready to take your parrot for car rides, you should also do this in steps. Start with a short ride around the block; if your parrot is comfortable, try longer rides.

Harness Training

If you want to take your parrot outside for walks or to explore, a harness is an excellent tool for keeping him safe. Even if he has had his wings clipped, it is a good idea to keep him restrained. Many a parrot that was clipped has flown off because a few feathers had grown in and he found just the right wind to get lift. It is a dangerous world out there for a parrot, so it is better to be safe than sorry. Many people do not use harnesses, because their parrots refuse to let them put one on and chew at it. However, with some training you can get your bird to allow you to slip it right on and take him into the great outdoors.

Props Needed: Harness.

Cue: Presentation of the harness.

Desired Behavior: Parrot holds still and calmly accepts the harness being put on him.

Steps:

1. Parrot looks at harness.
2. Approaches harness.
3. Puts head through harness.
4. Allows harness to touch body.
5. Allows harness to lie on body.
6. Allows slipping of harness over one wing.
7. Allows slipping of harness over other wing.

Harness Wearing Tip

Even though your parrot cannot fly away if he is wearing a harness, he can still get into trouble. Hawks, cats, dogs, coyotes, and other predators can appear out of nowhere and take a swipe at your parrot if he is outside. If you are not close enough to him, you may not be able to help. And if you leave his lead long enough and aren't mindful of your surroundings, he can get tangled in trees and other objects. You should be close at hand and paying attention whenever you have your parrot out in his harness.

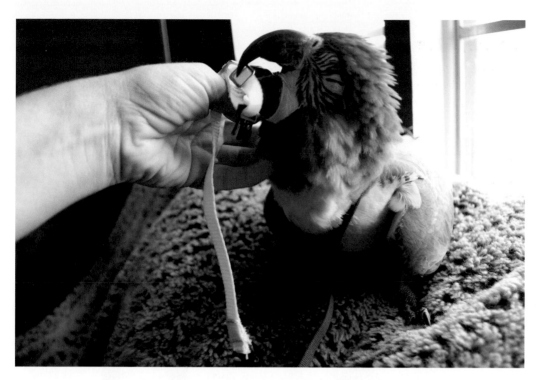

If you have a cuddly parrot, you can reward him with head scratches as you manipulate his body into the harness.

8. Allows tightening harness.
9. Comfortable with leaving harness on for extended period of time.

Instructions

If you have a parrot that is highly tactile and finds being cuddled and scratched extremely reinforcing, training him to wear a harness is fairly easy. A parrot that has this sort of personality or is young and still very cuddly does not mind letting you manipulate his body a little and move his wings. Move through all the steps using a scratch on the head instead of treats. Go slowly and make sure the parrot is comfortable, but the training should go quickly if you keep it positive.

If you have a parrot that does not like to be touched or is older and more

If your parrot gets fussy with the harness, you can distract him by cuing other behaviors he knows, such as stationing.

standoffish, you can still train him to wear a harness. You will need to use treats and take the training much more slowly in smaller approximations. Start by rewarding your parrot for staying when you hold out the harness, then for looking at and approaching the harness. This should be fairly easy if your parrot has not had any negative experiences with a harness.

Next hold the harness so that the opening is in front of your parrot and he can easily slip his head through. Using your target hand, get him to put his head through and give him a treat. He will probably pull his head right back out, which is fine. Get him to repeat the behavior and continue repetitions until he puts his head inside the harness without hesitation. While you do this, be careful that he does not get tangled in the harness; help him out of it if he gets snagged. Getting tangled in the harness would be a negative experience for your bird and likely will set your training back.

Once your parrot is confident putting his head into the harness, work on getting him to allow you to rest the harness on him. Reward him for this and lift it off if he shows any sign of discomfort. Move through the approximations of his allowing you to leave the harness draped over his head until he is leaving it on long enough for you to work on getting one loop over one of his wings.

You may have to reward him for letting you touch his wing, then to move it a bit and then to lift it up. When he is comfortable with you manipulating his wing, slip the loop over it. Keep the loops that go over the wing large, so that you only have to slip a loop under the wing and it can come off easily. This can be a little tricky, because if he is uncomfortable you need to help him get the harness back off. If he gets tangled and you have a little bit of an incident, that is okay. It isn't ideal, but it also is not the end of the world. Go back to the beginning of the behavior and give him some repetitions, starting at the beginning to get him back on track. At this point he should have enough history of positive reinforcement with the harness that he will be forgiving and let you try again.

When your parrot will let you slip the harness over his head, then over one wing, reinforce him for slipping it over the second wing. At this point he should be taking reinforcement and wearing it loosely with comfort. Now reinforce him for letting you tighten it. Do not tighten it all the way—just enough that it feels more snug. Then take it off again. Work on getting it cinched down a little tighter each time so that he is wearing it and ready to go out.

If your parrot does fuss with the harness once he is letting you put it on, you can distract him. Redirect him with your target hand. Move him around and even station him. Ask for behaviors he has been trained to do to redirect his attention, and then remove the harness. Don't forget to train him to sit still while you take the harness off as well. You will follow all the same steps, only backwards. After training, your parrot should happily allow you to put the harness on, especially when he learns that the harness means getting outside and doing something fun!

Potty Training

One of the biggest complaints parrot owners have is about their parrots' bathroom habits. Parrot leave droppings when and where they please in most houses, and people who are used to house-trained dogs and cats that use litter boxes do not appreciate it. What most people do not realize is that you can potty train your parrot fairly easily. It takes some time, requires knowing your parrot's body language, and means paying attention to him at all times when he is out of the cage. However, training only requires capturing the behavior (Capturing is explained below). If you make the effort to potty train, you will be glad you did.

Props Needed: None

Cue: Physical cue, placing on the station and verbal cue of "Go potty".

Desired Behavior: Parrot is placed in designated place and eliminates on cue.

Steps:

1. Parrot is placed in designated place to eliminate and cued.
2. Parrot eliminates waste and is rewarded.

Instructions

The way to "capture" a behavior is to watch for it and reward it when it happens. With some behaviors, like talking, you have to work on getting your bird to offer the behavior before you pair it with a cue. Fortunately, food moves through a parrot's digestive tract very quickly, and most parrot have to eliminate every 20 minutes or so. For smaller birds elimination can be even more frequent. So you can be fairly certain that you can capture this behavior at certain intervals.

Even better, most parrots give you some indication that they are going to eliminate. They may move foot to foot, act a little antsy, hunch and fluff out the feathers around the vent. Larger parrots are more obvious about it than smaller parrots, but if you watch you will learn and notice the "I've got to go potty" body language. Once you recognize this, you can interrupt your bird, distracting him with a noise, such as saying "Wait" and moving him to where you want him to go potty.

Once you have your parrot in the designated potty zone, you can cue him to go. The zone can be back in his cage, over a newspaper, or over a trashcan, but keep it consistent while you are training him. Once he is there cue him by saying,

"Go potty," and when he goes mark the event and give him a scratch on the head or reward him with a treat. If you do this consistently your parrot will learn to give you bigger signs that he needs to go. If he talks, he might even let you know by saying the cue "Go potty." He may still have accidents, but for the most part you will able to avoid having parrots dropping in places you do not want them to, like on your shoulder.

Conclusion

All of these behaviors should make living with a parrot more fun for you and make life less stressful and more enjoyable for your parrot. A parrot that is comfortable with being groomed, being handled by his avian vet, and wearing a harness is a parrot that is going to have a lot of enjoyable adventures. Also, you won't be worried that your parrot is stressed. And having a parrot that knows where to "go" is a big bonus. So now that you have some helpful training under your belt, let's train some fun stuff!

Potty Training Tip

As handy as potty training is, it is not a behavior that you want to be adamant about. Try not to make reinforcements big for going potty on cue. It is possible your parrot could learn to hold it until you cue him to go even when he really needs to go. If you have not cued him for hours, this could be very unhealthy for your parrot.

What Can Grey Do for You?

Some years ago I went back to graduate school as an excuse to write, to work at home, and to hang out with the parrots. And hang out with the parrots, I did! I spent three years working on my MFA and writing for a living. I was home most of the time, polishing my hermit ways. I hid myself away and tried to go out as little as possible. I ordered everything I could online. The UPS guy became my lifeline to the world.

I'll admit it. I loved my UPS guy. The brown shorts are part of it, but mostly it was just that he was the perfect boyfriend. He showed up nearly every day heralded by the distinct sound of his truck braking and a quick honk of the horn. (Antecedent) I would race to the door to meet him. (Behavior) He would stay just long enough to flirt with me, give me a present that I wanted (I had ordered it, after all) and then best of all, leave before his welcome was worn out. (Consequence) He wasn't just the perfect boyfriend. He was a wonderful trainer.

So the day I heard the brakes and the horn, raced across the house to throw open the door for my beloved and found no one there, I began to think it might be time to go back to an office job. I wondered if hallucinations were a given when you spent as much time alone in your imagination as I had been doing of late. I promised myself I would have dinner with a friend and get out of the house. Then I went back to my hidey-hole, emerging only when I heard a braking truck and a cheerful honk.

There was no one there. Again.

I grumbled on my way back to the article I was working on. I should probably go to the movies as well as dinner. And maybe I should invite a couple of friends over. An hour or so later, immersed in website copy, I heard the tell-tale sounds of UPS Guy once more. I sat for a moment, asking myself whether I had really heard him and certain I had. Still, I approached the front door cautiously, unsurprised when I opened it and found nobody there and no package. Surely I had cracked at last. Or had I?

I turned to look at my African grey parrot, Ty, whose cage was positioned in a see-the-whole-world spot in the living room, and it suddenly all made sense. He had learned to execute a spot-on imitation of the UPS truck. I was certain of it when he began to laugh.

I don't know that he thought this was funny, but I'm sure he watched the expressions play across my face: wonder, certainty, anger, and then amusement. We laughed together. Really, what better parrot enrichment than training his human? Ty had figured out the antecedent that was likely to make me come running. I'm a bigger challenge than training the dog, but I had still been had.

6

Advanced Fun:
The Next Steps
in Training

Some of the most complicated behaviors you can train are built upon simple behaviors. For example, there are many behaviors that can be trained when a parrot understands how to target. As you train some of these behaviors you may think of some new and fun behaviors to train on your own. That is the joy of training. The possibilities are limited only by your imagination. Let's start with a couple of easy tricks to train to get you started.

The Wave

Training the wave is one of the quickest tricks you can train, but it is always a crowd pleaser. This is a great way for both you and your parrot to gain confidence in trick training.

Props Needed: None
Cue: Verbal cue of wave and physical cue of wiggling right index finger.
Desired Behavior: Parrot lifts foot up in air, appearing to wave "Hello".
Steps:
1. Parrot begins to lift foot as if to step up when perch hand is presented.
2. Lifts foot up half an inch.

The trick to teaching the wave is to mark and reward when he lifts up his foot but before he actually steps on your hand.

3. Lifts foot up an inch.
4. Lifts foot up to beak.
5. Parrot lifts foot to cue even though hand is just out of reach to step up onto.
6. Lifts foot even though hand is not moving in for a step-up.
7. Lifts foot for wave on cue of finger wiggle and saying "Wave".

Instructions

Teaching a parrot to wave on cue is fairly simple and can often be trained in one or two sessions. The challenging part of training a wave is marking the behavior at the right moment so that you can shape it correctly. You have to have excellent timing with your clicker or your verbal marker. If you do not quite have the timing down for using an event marker yet, this is an excellent way to practice and learn.

It is fairly easy to teach your parrot to wave on cue.

Start by holding up your hand as if to step up your parrot. Move in just close enough that your parrot shifts his weight onto one foot and starts to move to step up. You want to say "good" the moment the foot heading toward your hand leaves the perch. If you mark that event too late your parrot will think that you are rewarding the step-up. Cue him by saying "wave," while wiggling the right index finger on your target hand. Slowly move your perch hand in and catch him just as he is lifting his foot, mark it, and reward him.

Your parrot will likely be watching your target hand and the cue. So when you move your perch hand in for the step-up, he may absently lift his foot. This will slow him down a bit and make it easier for you to catch him lifting his foot and say "good" at the right moment.

Next try to get him to lift his foot a little higher without stepping up onto your hand, mark it, and reward it. Keep making small steps with him, getting his foot higher until he lifts it all the way up to the height of his chest.

Once you have your parrot lifting his foot up to his beak when you move your perch hand in, stop moving your perch hand in as close. You are going to start phasing out the perch hand and get your parrot to wave when you cue him with your index finger. Move your perch hand in so that it is just out of reach for a step-up, say "Wave," wiggle your right index finger, and get him to lift his foot.

Once he is lifting his foot just out of reach, cue him with your hand farther and farther out of reach until you can leave your perch hand out altogether. Getting to this point will happen quickly when your parrot understands that he is being rewarded for raising his foot. You may even be able to train this behavior in just one session.

Training Game

One of the best things you can do to learn what it is like for your parrot and to increase your training prowess is to play the training game. Get together a group of people and send one person outside the room; this person will be "the parrot." Then decide what behavior you are going to train your "parrot" and choose a trainer. Keep it fairly simple. Something like, "walk in the room, pick up the blue notebook from the table, and put it on that chair" is about as complicated as you should get. Then call the "parrot" back in the room.

In order to train the subject, the trainer will only be using claps. Use just one clap whenever your subject is getting close or begins to make a movement that is part of the behavior. The closer the subject gets, the faster and louder you clap. When the subject gets off track, stop clapping. Do this without using any sounds from the trainer or the audience. No groaning or cheers and no hand signals, head movements, or giving hints with your eyes either. For example, when your subject comes into the room, clap, but then stop clapping until she moves in the direction of the notebook, then start clapping again. When she gets to the table, clap when she reaches out. She will probably start reaching out for different things. Stop clapping as she reaches out in the wrong direction, but clap again when her hand moves toward the notebook. In this way you shape the behavior and in a fun way realize the perils and pitfall of training without language and shared body language. Plus, it's just plain fun.

Capturing a Wave

Another way you can train this behavior is to capture it. If you have a parrot that frequently touches his beak with his foot you can watch for this behavior and reward it. In the evening when you are watching television or doing something that allows you to keep an eye on your parrot, wait for your bird to lift his foot to his beak, mark the event, and then get up and reward him. Again the timing of marking the event is critical. You must say "good" right when his foot is touching his beak. The first couple of times you reward him he will likely be mystified. Then the light in his head will come on and he will begin to offer the behavior. Once he is offering it, you can start using the cue and rewarding him only when he offers it after the cue. Capturing a wave is a bit more challenging than shaping it if you don't have a lot of time to wait for your parrot to offer it, but it is good know and fun to try a variety of ways to train behaviors.

You can train your parrot to turn around by targeting either below the stand or above his head.

Turning Around

Training a parrot to turn in a circle is perhaps another one of the simplest behaviors to train. If you have been feeling a bit frustrated with your attempts, this behavior should get your confidence back on track. It will also give your parrot a chance to succeed and get lots of positive reinforcement

> **Props Needed:** A perch that is at chest level and allows you to reach underneath.
> **Cue:** Verbal cue of "Turn" and physical cue of moving target hand in circular motion.
> **Desired Behavior:** Parrot turns whole body in circle.

Steps:

1. Parrot targets to closed hand.
2. Follows, targeting closed hand to turn head.
3. Targets hand, turning 90 degrees.
4. Targets hand, turning 180 degrees.
5. Targets hand, turning 270 degrees.
6. Targets hand, turning in a full circle, 360 degrees.
7. Turns 360 degreeswith target hand leading only at stages.
8. Targets turning 360 degrees with hand moving too fast to be "luring" parrot.
9. Turns 360 degrees with just a circular motion of hand cuing parrot.
10. Turns 360 degrees with very minimal circular motion of hand.

Instructions

This behavior is easiest to train if you have a T-stand or a U-shaped stand. Either of these makes it possible to move your hand underneath the bird. If your parrot has

Evolving Behaviors

A behavior is never completely trained. Once your parrot understands a behavior you have taught him, be sure to set your criteria for that behavior and stick to them. If your criterion for targeting is to have your parrot touch the target with his beak, keep it that way. Behaviors evolve even after they are trained. If you relax your expectations and reward your parrot for just getting close to the target, that is all you are going to get, and the behavior will continue to get sloppier. Then if suddenly you decide to reward your parrot only if he touches the target, you will have a frustrated parrot that has had the rules changed on him. You also have to remember to reward the desired behavior fairly often. As you begin to train more complicated behavior, this will become even more important. Remember that the training never ends entirely, because behavior is not static. If you become a sloppy trainer, your parrot will give you sloppy behavior.

a stand on top of his cage that is not any higher than your shoulders, this can also work. If you use the T-stand frequently when you train, your parrot will know that it is time to train when he is placed on it.

Place your parrot on the perch and get his attention with your target hand. Use the verbal cue "Turn" if you wish, or you can use just the physical cue of presenting and encouraging the parrot to follow the target. Put your target hand below him so that he cannot quite reach it, but leans toward it. Get him to turn his head toward your hand. Mark the event and reward him. Next, cue him to target, bringing him to turn his body as far as he can without turning his feet, mark the event, and reward him.

The next step is to get him to follow your target hand so that he turns to face the opposite direction. Keep moving him a little farther until you can get him to turn all the way around by leading him with the target. This may happen very quickly, and you may find that your approximations do not have to be as small as I have made them here. It is always best to have the smallest approximations in mind, because you can always skip through them quickly if your parrot is thinking fast on his feet.

Once you have your parrot turning in a full circle to follow the target without hesitation, begin to phase out the target. Move your hand a bit faster than the parrot so that he is turning to reach the target but not being dragged along by it. Continue to make the revolution of your hand faster until just reaching forward gets your parrot to begin to turn. Then whittle down your movements to a small circle made with your hand in front of the perch. If at any time your parrot gets stuck and stops turning with your hand, back up a few steps and get him to follow the target. This behavior can be trained very quickly; you may even be able to get it down in one training session.

Alternative Way to Train the Turn

If you do not have a perch that you can reach underneath, you can still train the turn by targeting above your parrot's head. I prefer to train with my hand below the parrot because it is more comfortable for me and the parrot. Some parrots can be intimidated by a hand or target hovering above them. If you have a parrot that is new to you and nervous of your movements, I do not recommend training this

At first, reward your parrot when he just approaches the tube.

way. However, if your parrot is very comfortable with you and shows no signs of moving away or flinching when you reach above him, training this way will work as well.

Using a target that will keep you from hovering above the parrot too much, position the target in front of him and lead him around the perch, following all the same steps listed above. Once he will turn all the way around with minimal guidance from the target, switch out the target for your index finger. Once he is comfortable with your finger as the target, move the cue from above him to in front of him and change the cue to a quick circle with your finger when you say "Turn". Either method will get you the same behavior, so choose whichever is more comfortable for both you and the parrot.

Through a Tunnel

Many parrots naturally enjoy crawling into and around small spaces, and running through a tunnel is fun and easy for them. Most people do not realize this is a natural behavior, though, and are surprised to see a parrot ramble through a small opening and pop out the other side. It is a cute trick, especially if it is a component of a full obstacle course.

Props Needed: Cardboard tube big enough for your parrot to move through

Cue: Verbal cue of "Tunnel" and physical cue of pointing to cardboard tube

Desired Behavior: Parrot goes in one end of the tube and comes out the other

Steps:

1. Parrot looks at tube.
2. Touches inside of tube.
3. Puts head inside tube.
4. Takes several steps into tube.
5. Gets to the middle of the tube.
6. Climbs all the way through tube.

Instructions

You may need to find several sizes of cardboard tubes (an empty paper towel roll works for the smallest birds, but you will need to find a larger tube for other

When your parrot goes through the tube without hesitating you can phase out the target and only use a verbal or gestural cue.

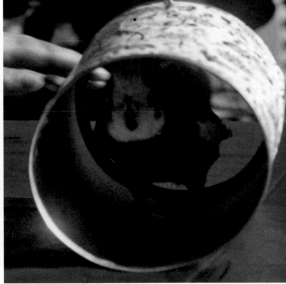

parrots) or create your own so that your parrot fits comfortably through the tube. For the most part parrots are very comfortable with going through a tube because they are cavity nesters and going through narrow openings is natural for them. If it turns out your parrot is nervous, though, you can start with a very large tube and then train the next size smaller and the next size smaller and so on until your parrot happily trots in and out of a small tube. You should train this behavior on the floor or on a table.

Make sure the tube is nontoxic for chewing and that there are no sharp points sticking out. When you start training, make sure the tube you are using is secure. Staple it or tape it to a piece of wood or something to steady it. If the tube rolls when your parrot is first learning to go in and out of it, this may startle him and make it difficult to continue to train. You always want to do whatever you can to keep the training positive and easy for the parrot.

You will need to use a target like a chopstick to get your parrot to approach the tube. At the end where you want him to enter, hold the target at the entrance. Cue him, mark the event, and reward him when he touches the target. Next, slide the target through the end he will be coming out of and get him to put his head into the tube a little way to touch the target. Say "good" and reward him.

Point to the entrance of the tube when you want him to go in and get him to target. Make small approximations, getting him farther and farther into the tube with the target. He will likely get part way in and back right out. This is fine. Reward him for going a little farther each time.

Once he gets halfway into the tube, try to lead him the rest of the way out with the target. Keep up with him; if he has forward motion, don't block him with the target—bring it all of the way out of the tube. Once he gets his whole body in, he is likely to want to come out the other side rather than back up.

When your parrot is going all the way through the tube, being led by the target, begin to phase the target out. Point to the entrance with your free hand, giving the cue and holding the target at the other end of the tube. Be careful that you do not block him on his way out. Hold the target farther and farther away from the end of the tube as you are cuing him to enter until you no longer need the target. At this point you should be able to point to the opening and get your parrot to run right through.

Climb the Rope

Like squeezing through a small space, climbing up a rope is also a natural behavior for a parrot. In the wild parrots are often hanging from thin branches and scrambling through trees playing. So training your parrot to climb up a rope with the target is a breeze. Your parrot may already have ropes he climbs on or in his cage or play area. All you have to do is train him to do it on cue.

Props Needed: Rope hanging from perch
Cue: Verbal "Climb" and physical cue of pointing to rope
Desired Behavior: Parrot climbs up rope and gets onto perch
Steps:

1. Parrot looks at rope.
2. Touches rope.
3. Puts foot onto rope.
4. Uses beak to climb one step up on rope.
5. Climbs several steps on rope.
6. Climbs all the way to perch on rope and climbs onto perch.
7. Parrot climbs up rope with minimal targeting.
8. Climbs up rope on cue.

Directions

Hang the rope from a sturdy perch that will give him a place to sit and get a treat once he climbs to the top. Then begin by using the target to get him to approach the rope.

Climbing up a rope is an easy behavior to train because it is something parrots do naturally.

Lead your parrot up the slide's ladder with small approximations until he is comfortable climbing up the ladder.

Next hold the target next to the rope and above his head so that he has to stretch to touch the target.

Now begin working on getting him to climb. You may be able to do this in a quick few steps. Cue him by telling him to "Climb" and pointing to the perch. In small approximations (unless he bolts right up the rope—and he may) get him to climb a bit farther each time until he gets to the perch.

Once your parrot is easily climbing up the rope and getting to the perch, begin to phase out the target. Stop leading him with the target and keep it farther in front of him until you can just hold it up at the perch. Ultimately you will get rid of it altogether. Depending on how high you are asking him to climb, climbing the rope should train quickly, taking only a couple of sessions. If you want, you also train him to climb back down using the same approximations in the opposite order and with a different cue such as "Down".

Down the Slide

While parrots do not tend to slide down slick surfaces much in the wild, parrots that have been trained to do this trick look as if they are having a great time on their tiny slides. This trick can take some effort to train because a parrot's natural tendency is often to jump off the slide. If you use small approximations your parrot will be zipping down the slide in no time.

Props Needed: Appropriately sized slide with ladder on one side.
Cue: Verbal "Slide" and physical cue of pointing to the slide.
Desired Behavior: Parrot climbs up the ladder and goes down the slide.
Steps:

1. Parrot looks at slide.
2. Parrot approaches slide.
3. Touches rung on ladder.
4. Puts foot onto rung.
5. Climbs a rung.
6. Climbs to top.
7. Steps onto slide.
8. Slides down slide.

Train with Friends

It is a great idea to find a group of friends locally or online who are also learning to train their parrots. People, like parrots, are social animals, and it is so much fun to share your successes. More than that, though, several heads are sometimes better than one. Even if you are not all experts, you can all share your experiences and help each other. If you get stuck training, a friend may see things that you don't or think of a clever way to shape a behavior that you might not think of yourself. Or perhaps your friend can explain something she has learned in a way that makes sense to you. And if you decide to attend workshops or conferences, you will have someone to go with and learn with you. If you enjoy socializing with other people, a group of friends with parrots can be a blast.

Getting your parrot to slide down the slide can be tricky; he may jump off or walk down instead of sliding.

9. Climbs up and slides down slide with minimal targeting.
10. Climbs up and slides down slide on cue.

Directions

Make sure the ladder is sturdy enough to hold your parrot without falling over and large enough that he can fit on it comfortably. You may need to secure the ladder to something to keep it from tipping. Unlike the previous two behaviors, sliding down things is not as natural, especially for some species of parrots. So this may take longer to train. You also may have some difficulty finding a ladder. There are some made for hamsters that will work for smaller birds, and you can also make your own if you are handy. Despite the fact that you may have some difficulties getting a ladder for your bird, it is such a cute behavior that I thought I would include it.

Start by targeting your parrot to approach the ladder. Once your parrot will approach the slide, hold your target hand over his head and next to the steps so that he has to stretch up in the direction of the target. Mark the event and reward him.

In the next step, try to get him to put a foot on the rungs and then climb up a bit. Shape the behavior of climbing the ladder in small approximations based on your parrot's abilities and confidence. Once your parrot reaches the top of the ladder, begin to work on getting him down the slide—this may be the trickiest part.

Cue your parrot; when he gets to the top of the ladder, begin to approximate him down. He will likely try to walk down the slide, and this is fine. As he becomes more comfortable and is motivated to complete the whole behavior for a treat, he will slide all the way down. Don't try asking him to move farther than he is comfortable because he may just jump off the slide. If he does jump off, don't mark the event and reward him. Start over and don't ask him to move as far down the slide.

Once he understands that the whole behavior is to climb up the ladder and go down the slide, target him only at stages instead of leading him with the target. Point to the ladder and say "Ladder" as a cue and phase out the target until you only have to target him at the end of the slide and then not at all. Your parrot should learn the slide in a few training sessions; when he gets the hang of it and slides all the way down the slide, it is a blast to watch.

How Much Training in a Day?

Believe it or not, training for 15 or 20 minutes a day to train a specific behavior is totally sufficient. If you want to train your parrot a trick, you do not have to spend several hours a day working on it. Your average training session is only going to last about 10 minutes and likely no longer than 20 minutes. One or two sessions a day is plenty. Your parrot is not going to forget what he has already learned. If you want to train more, you certainly can, but don't spend hours a day focused on training. Both you and your parrot are likely to get training fatigue, and no one wants that—training is supposed to be fun!

Behavior Chains

Once your parrot has learned all of the previous behaviors and does them on cue without hesitation, it is easy to chain all or some of them together. A behavior chain is a group of behaviors that an animal performs while getting a reward only at the end. You have probably seen behavior chains that have been trained in talking parrot routines or with props. If you have ever watched dog agility courses, these too are chained behaviors. Even the small things we ask our dogs to do in succession without reinforcement like "Come," "Sit," and "Stay" are behavior chains. This works because after training for a while your event marker becomes a secondary reinforcer.

The sound of the clicker or the word "good" quickly becomes rewarding to a parrot when he knows it means that a reward is coming. This is much like when children get excited when they hear the sound of the ice cream truck coming down the street. Even if they don't get ice cream, the link between the sound and the experience of getting ice cream and possibly getting it again makes it rewarding. Since the event marker is rewarding and the behaviors have a history of reinforcement and are on cue, they can be chained together.

If you want your parrot to do an obstacle course, train each behavior individually. Make sure you have instant response to the cue and that your parrot is confident with the whole behavior. You can then get your parrot to go through a tunnel, climb up the ladder and go down the slide, climb up the rope, and wave. After each behavior, click or say "good" and at the end of the chain of behaviors give him a sizable reward. When you are training the chained behaviors, add only one behavior at a time. You can switch around the order of the behaviors if you wish, but if you ask for the behaviors in the same order every time it will be easier for your parrot to learn to link them, and the chain will be less likely to break down.

Retrieve

Training a retrieve can take a little bit of time, but it is a great behavior that you can have a lot of fun with in a variety of applications. Once your parrot learns to pick something up and put it in the appropriate place, you can generalize this to various different activities. First, though, you need to teach your parrot how to pick up a toy and put it away.

Training your parrot to pick up an item and drop it in a designated place is the basis of several other fun tricks.

Props Needed: Metal bowl, poker chips, or some other practically indestructible small toy

Cue: Presentation of chip and bowl

Desired Behavior: Parrot takes the chip and drops it into the bowl

Steps:

1. Parrot looks at chip.
2. Takes chip.
3. Drops chip into bowl directly beneath him.
4. Drops chip into bowl just off to the side of him.
5. Leans to get chip into bowl.
6. Takes step to drop chip into bowl.
7. Takes several steps to drop chip into bowl.
8. Walks length of perch to drop chip into bowl.

Instructions

Training a retrieve may take several sessions because it is fairly complicated for your parrot to understand initially that you are rewarding him for taking something from you and then making an effort to drop it into the bowl. Make sure that the object you choose for retrieval is something your parrot is comfortable with and interested in. Of course, you also want to make sure it is something safe for your parrot to play with and chew on. An unused or cleaned poker chip works well for many parrots, but make sure that what you choose is appropriate for your parrot's size, easy to take from you, and easy to hold on to.

Place your parrot on a T-stand or similar perch and hold the metal bowl directly underneath him with your left hand. With your right hand, offer him the poker chip. Most likely he will take it from you right away, as parrots are prone to play with new and interesting things. If he does not take it, you may need to reward him for approaching it and then touching it. Once the parrot has taken the chip, wait for him to drop it, keeping the bowl underneath him. When the poker chip falls and hits the bowl, wait for the plunk of it hitting the bowl and then say "good" and reward him. Retrieve the chip while he is eating his treat and start again.

Juggling the bowl, the chip, and the food in your hand takes some coordination, but you will get the hang of it. Keep your treats small because you will want to move through the approximations quickly. Hand your parrot the chip again, and wait for him to drop it again. Mark and reward when the chip hits the bowl. Do this several times so that hopefully your parrot starts to associate the marked event as having something to do with the bowl.

Next you will want to move the bowl slightly to the side of your parrot. If he misses, say nothing, pick up the chip, and try again. Missing is as important as getting the chip into the bowl because it gives your parrot an idea of why he is and is not being reinforced. If he gets it in by accident, be sure to reward that as well. Even getting the chip into the bowl by accident counts, because at this stage of the game you are just trying to communicate what you are looking for, which is the plunk of the chip into the metal bowl.

Once your parrot is obviously leaning to put the chip in the bowl, move it an inch or so farther away. If your parrot takes the chip, drops it, and misses more than a couple of times, move the bowl back underneath him and let him succeed. This way he will not get frustrated. Understanding that the goal is to get the chip into the bowl is challenging the first time. You will need to be patient. Keep moving forward in small approximations and soon you will be able to get him to walk down the length of the perch and put the chip into the bowl.

When your parrot understands the retrieve on the perch, try giving him some other items to drop into the bowl. Introduce him to only one item at a time, and take a few steps back in the training to set him up to succeed. This will teach him to generalize.

Fun Ways to Retrieve

Once you have taught your parrot to retrieve, you can teach him to do a few fun tricks. To set him up for learning to retrieve, get out your poker chips and metal bowl. Place your parrot on a table with room for him to move around. Hand him a poker chip and then hold out the bowl. If he does not understand right away, hold the bowl underneath him, say "good" when he drops the chip into it, and reward him. Then set the bowl down on the table and give your parrot the chip. Using small approximations, get him to walk the length of the table to deposit the chip into the bowl. Since he already knows this, he should pick it up in just a few steps.

The first step to training the basketball trick is to get your parrot to pick up the ball.

Once he is picking up the ball, use your target hand to lead him to the basket.

Ultimately, your parrot will pick up the ball, take it to the basket, and drop it in on cue.

Next set the chip down on the table. You want to try to get him to pick it up and put it into the bowl. He may do it right away. If he doesn't, then target him to the chip. If he still hesitates about picking up, say "good" and reward him for touching it. When he does this a couple of times, start saying "good" and rewarding only when he tries to pick it up. When he finally picks it up, get him to put it into the bowl. Once he understands that the retrieve happens on the table, you can introduce him to new props.

Basketball

Everyone has probably seen parrots playing basketball at a bird show or on television. This behavior is a crowd pleaser, and it is not that hard to train, especially if your parrot already knows how to retrieve. Plus it is a great way for an active parrot to burn off energy and play.

Props Needed: Ball and basketball hoop (You can buy these specifically for parrots; check your local bird or pet store or search online.)
Cue: Verbal cue of "Dunk it" and physical cue of presentation of ball and basket
Desired Behavior: Parrot picks up the ball, walks over to the basket, and dunks the ball in.

Steps:

1. Parrot looks at the ball.
2. Touches ball.
3. Takes ball.
4. Holds ball, turns to follow target.
5. Holds ball, follows target to basket.
6. Carries ball to basket following target, touches ball to basket.
7. Drops ball into basket.

Instructions

Check around on the Internet for basketball sets designed for parrots. There are a few places where you can purchase them. In general, you may have to be inventive when it comes to props for training, but the Web is a good place to start. Make sure that the ball has holes in it so that your parrot can pick it up easily; something similar to a Wiffle ball works well. Also make sure that the basket is not easily tipped over; you may have to secure it for training.

Place the basket, the ball, and your parrot on a table with plenty of room to

Let Go

If you decide to train a lot of behaviors that involve props, you may want to train your parrot to "Let go." Parrots love to play, and if your parrot grabs a prop when you are training, you don't want to fight him for it. Let him play with it. However, this can get distracting and slow training sessions down if your parrot decides he wants to play for some time. Training your parrot to let go of what he has is easy. When it looks as if he is about to lose interest in what he has in his feet, say "Let go" and repeat it until he drops the prop. Then say "good" and give him a treat. By doing this you are capturing the behavior. Your parrot will quickly learn that he gets a reward for dropping what is in his feet if you say "Let go." Of course, if what he is playing with is more interesting than the treat you are offering, you'll still have to wait a bit, but the "Let go" cue will definitely speed things up.

maneuver. Put the ball right next to the basket. Target your parrot to the ball. If he immediately picks it up, say "good" and give him a treat. If he doesn't pick it up right away, get him to look at it, touch it, and then pick it up.

Once your parrot is picking up the ball, use your target hand to lead him to the basket. Start by rewarding him for moving toward the basket with the ball in his mouth. Then reward him for touching the ball to the basket, and then for making an effort to get the ball into the basket. Once he understands that the reward is for getting the ball into the basket, you can move the ball farther and farther away. Pretty soon your parrot will be playing ball!

Piggy Bank

Training a parrot to put coins into a piggy bank is one of my favorite tricks. This is a wonderful trick for some of the smaller species such as Senegal parrots, conures, and pionus. Some parrots can keep themselves occupied for long periods of time when given a stack of coins to bank.

> **Props Needed:** Piggy bank and plastic coins that fit in the slot.
> **Cue:** Pointing to coins; presence of coins and bank will ultimately be the cue
> **Desired Behavior:** Parrot picks up coins and slips them into the slot on the piggy bank.
> **Steps:**
> 1. Parrot looks at the coin.
> 2. Touches coin.
> 3. Takes coin.
> 4. Holds coin, turns to follow target.
> 5. Holds coin, follows target to piggy bank.
> 6. Carries coin to bank following target, touches coin to bank.
> 7. Touches coin to slot.
> 8. Drops coin into slot.

Instructions

Find a small sturdy piggy bank that is the right size for your parrot. You will want one that he can stand above with a coin in his beak and easily slip into the slot.

Plastic coins are best if you can find them. You can use regular money, but if you do, be sure to clean and disinfect it. Who knows where your change has been while in circulation?

Train this the same way you would train basketball. It will be a little more challenging to get your parrot to fit the coins into the slot, however. Once you have your parrot carrying the coin over to the top of the piggy bank, reward him for getting closer and closer to fitting it in. Each time he drops the coin, pick it up and slip it into the slot so he can see how it fits. You will want to have a handful of plastic coins available to keep things moving.

Training your parrot to put coins in a piggy bank is very similar to training him to put a basketball through a hoop.

Most parrots seem to enjoy putting small objects inside larger ones and pick this trick up with ease. However, if your parrot has trouble with it you can use approximations to help him learn to fit a coin into a smaller hole. Make a small box with several tops. The first top should have a large hole the coin can easily be dropped into. Then switch to a top that is smaller and, when your parrot is confidently putting coins into the slot, change to a top that is as small as the piggy bank slot. Once he has this down, you can switch over to the piggy bank. This is an entertaining behavior to watch. There are tons of videos on the Internet of parrots putting their savings away into banks if you want to see what this looks like before you train it.

Pull the Wagon

Training a parrot to pull a small wagon with his beak can be a great trick to add to a routine. I have seen routines where one parrot has even been trained to

You can train your parrot to drop an object into the wagon before he pulls it by chaining the two behaviors together.

jump into the wagon and ride while another parrot pulls. It is a cute behavior and something different to train a parrot that has already mastered retrieving.

Props Needed: Parrot-sized wagon or cart on wheels.

Cue: Verbal cue of "Pull the wagon" and physical cue of pointing to wagon.

Desired Behavior: Parrot grabs hold of wagon handle and pulls it.

Steps:

1. Parrot looks at wagon.
2. Moves toward wagon.
3. Touches wagon.
4. Touches wagon handle.
5. Holds on to wagon handle.
6. Tugs at wagon handle.
7. Hold on to wagon handle and follows target hand to take a step.
8. Follows target hand to pull wagon several steps.
9. Pull wagon to target hand.

Directions

Find a small wagon or cart that is easy for your parrot to move. Place it on a table or floor with lots of room to maneuver, and make sure the wagon can roll easily on the surface. Just as with all the other behaviors, take your time and make sure that your parrot is not afraid of the wagon before you start working with him.

Point to the wagon to cue him and then, using your target hand, get your parrot to approach the wagon, mark the event, and reward him. Get him closer with each approximation until you can get him to touch the handle. Once he is touching the handle, reward him for holding it in his beak for a couple of seconds.

Next you will want to get him to move it. Chances are he will tug on the handle as he is investigating the new toy. Even if he pulls on the wagon's handle by accident, be sure to say "good" and reward him. You can capture the behavior of him moving the wagon this way and then begin to shape it into pulling the wagon for a distance.

If your parrot is not pulling on the wagon's handle, point to the wagon handle to cue him and use your treat hand to target him to turn his head while he has the handle. The wagon will move when he turns his head, and you can mark the event and reward him. Now get him to move and follow your target hand a step with the wagon handle in his beak. Mark the event and reward, then continue to shape the behavior with small approximations until your parrot will take several steps with the wagon.

Superstitious Behaviors

Sometimes unintended behaviors are accidentally created when we are training something else. This can happen by not marking the event or reinforcing at the right time. For example, let's say you are training your parrot to lift his wings. Right before he starts to lift his wings, he drops his head and you say "good" and reward him. So when you cue him next, he drops his head and you wait a bit longer and he starts to lift his wings and you reward him. For a while and maybe even from there on out, he will drop his head and then lift his wings unless you train him otherwise. He thinks that the head drop is part of the behavior. This is called a superstitious behavior. Most of the time superstitious behaviors are not a problem, but they are easy to accidentally train, so you should be mindful of the possibility.

Start by leading him to where you want him to go with your target hand, and then phase out the target. You should be able to point to the wagon and then hold your target hand at the spot where you want your parrot to bring the wagon.

If you want to make this trick extra fun you can use the retrieve behavior to train him to put something into the wagon and then pull it. Chain all these behaviors together and you have a mini parrot show. Whether or not you entertain guests at your dinner parties or post videos on YouTube, you are likely to have a tremendous amount of fun training. Your parrot will also have the benefit of exercise, enriching ways to use his brain power, and quality time you!

Physical Tricks

If you have a parrot that is extremely comfortable with being handled, there are some behaviors you can train that involve getting him to position his body. A parrot that loves to be cuddled and to have your hands all over him will be especially easy to train this way. Also with a parrot that finds tactile interaction rewarding, you can reward with scratches and cuddles instead of treats. If you have a cuddly bird that just isn't very food motivated, these are a couple of tricks that will be perfect for you to try out.

Make sure that your parrot is completely comfortable with you before you train these tricks as described. If you have a parrot that is not comfortable with being touched, you could still train them, but you will need to think through some strategies you can use that involve targeting and very small approximations. Every parrot is an individual, and the best way to learn may be different for each individual. If your parrot does not like being handled, you could do serious damage to your

Skipping Steps

By the time you have trained several behaviors with props you will likely find that your parrot immediately approaches new props with interest, ready to find out what he is going to learn to do. At this point you will be able to skip the steps of having the parrot look and approach the prop. He will do this on his own with no prompting. However, these steps are always good to keep in mind. You never know when something about a new prop might not sit well with your parrot. If he is frightened of it and not desensitized, you may have a big setback in training.

Refresher Course

When you start a new training session it is a good idea to set your parrot up to succeed and to build confidence with a refresher course. Rather than starting right where you left off in training the behavior, start at the beginning and quickly run through to where you left off. For example, if you are training your parrot to wear a harness and you left off at tightening the harness, begin again at targeting your parrot through the opening and run him through the steps. This gives your parrot an opportunity to remember what you were doing and to get some positive reinforcement right away, before the training gets a little more challenging.

relationship by training this way. However, if your parrot will let you do just about anything with him, have fun! These are just a couple of tricks you can train.

Eagle

Some parrots, like cockatoos, are real naturals at stretching out and showing off their wing span. No matter the species, training a parrot to put out his wings and look like an "eagle" can be really stunning and show off his colors.

Props Needed: None

Cue: Verbal "Eagle"

Desired Behavior: Parrot lifts wings up and holds them there.

Steps:

1. Parrot allows you to move finger toward wings.
2. Allows you to touch wings.
3. Allows you scratch under wings with index finger.
4. Lifts wing an inch when you scratch under wings.
5. Lifts both wings up when you scratch under both.
6. Lifts wings halfway.
7. Lifts wings all the way up.
8. Raises wings up and holds them there.

Instructions

With your parrot sitting on a perch, move your index finger to scratch under the wings. If he has never been scratched under his wings before, take the time to go slowly and train this behavior. With a bird that is very tactile, it's likely you've scratched under the wings before. So when you move to scratch under a wing and he lifts it up, stop, say "good," and give him a scratch on the head or other reward he values.

Continue with getting him to lift the one wing until he is lifting it somewhat without hesitation and then try scratching under both wings. Cue him saying "Eagle" and then reach to scratch under his wings, approximating so that each time he gets his wings a little higher before you say "good" and then cuddle him.

Once he is lifting his wings all the way up, begin to phase out your cue. Instead of reaching all the way in to scratch, stop right before his wings. When he consistently lifts his wing when you do this, move back six inches, then a foot, and so on until you are just pointing with both fingers. Then move to just one finger. If you are also saying "Eagle" as the cue, you can then eliminate the physical cue altogether and just use the verbal cue.

Training your parrot to spread out his wings like an eagle is a fun way to show off his colors.

As you are shaping this behavior, you should also watch how your parrot positions his head. If his head is down and you would rather that he held his head up high as well as his wings, make sure that this is what you reinforce. When you use your event marker and give him a treat, he will think that his positioning is exactly what you are rewarding. So make sure you are rewarding what you want.

Play Dead

Teaching a parrot to play dead requires a lot of trust and more touching than the eagle behavior. Go slowly and carefully while training this and make sure your parrot is never uncomfortable with the step you are currently training. Train this only with a parrot that lets you put your hands all over him when you play and cuddle.

Props Needed: None
Cue: Verbal "Play dead"
Desired Behavior: Parrot lies on back for several seconds without moving
Steps:
1. Parrot stands on your perch hand.
2. Allows you to place your hand on his back.
3. Allows you to keep your hand on his back.
4. Lets you tip him backward slightly with your hand on his back.

It's critical when training the play dead that your parrot be comfortable and not frightened. The parrot on the left is nervous and struggling. The one on the right is comfortable and relaxed.

5. Lets you tip him at an angle backwards.
6. Holds still as you tip him all the way onto his back.
7. Holds still on his back without holding on to your fingers.
8. Stays on his back with his feet up while you move him.
9. Stays in position when you place him on a table.
10. Stays in position on a table until you say "good" or click.

Instructions

With your parrot on your perch hand, place your hand on his back. If he is comfortable with this, begin to lean him backward just slightly. If he struggles at all or tenses up, immediately put him upright. Try to get him back just a little so you can mark the event with "good" and then reward him with a head scratch. Most parrots are going to be a little nervous about being on their backs for the first time, so train this with extremely small approximations. Get him backwards a little at a time.

When he is comfortable going all the way backward and lying in your hand with his feet up, see whether you can get him to stay in this position for a few seconds. If he wants up, let him get back up. Do not force him to stay in this position. You want to keep the training positive.

When your parrot will let you put him on his back and stay in that position while holding on to your finger, work on getting him to let go of your fingers. If you have trained him to "Let go" (earlier in this chapter) this is a great time to use this behavior. Otherwise just wait for him let go or slowly loosen his grip by turning your finger. When he lets go say "good" and let him get back up and cuddle him.

The first couple of times he lets go, he is likely to reach out for your finger again. Let him grab it. He will be more comfortable at first with something in his feet while he is on his back. Work on this until you can cue him by saying "Play dead" and get him to lie flat on your hand, with his feet up in the air, and stay still until you say "good" and get him back up for scratches on the head or however he likes to be cuddled.

You can either end the behavior here or continue your approximations by getting him to lie comfortably while you move him. Next get him to hold the "play dead" position while you place him on the table, and then have him stay in position until you say "good" and reward him. With a parrot that allows you to manipulate his body, this can be a quick and easy train and a real crowd-pleasing trick as well! It is also a great way to build confidence with your parrot as long as you are mindful of his body language and allow him to dictate how fast the training goes. He will learn that you are responsive to him when he is uncomfortable or nervous and that he can trust you.

Conclusion

This is only a small sample of the tricks you can train your parrot to do. Once you have trained a few of them you may find yourself conjuring up a variety of tricks that your parrot will excel at learning. If you have a parrot that is also a chatterbox, you may also want to train him to talk and get some things on cue. We'll talk about vocal behaviors in the next chapter.

The final form of the play dead is a bird that lies limp or flat on his back with his feet in the air.

You Can Take It with You

In 1998 I went to Australia for six months. I had met a couple of Australians who had infected my imaginings with daydreams of Aussie raptors that haunted the bush and stole your heart. I wanted to go more than anything I had wanted before. There was just one problem, Ty. I was going to have to leave Ty behind for months.

Now, before you feel sorry for him, I worked at that time for a company that did free-flight bird shows. My options for where Ty might stay were huge and highly acceptable. In the end the decision was to situate him at "The Ranch" surrounded by trainers and enrichment in the form of other birds and constant toys. He would be just fine without me. And that was the problem.

Pining for a lost mate until you die is not a good survival strategy. I imagined Ty might wonder and maybe even miss me for a bit, but it would be much like the conure said in the movie *Polly*, "And one day, the cat got her." I was sure he was going to fall in love with someone else.

I adored Australia. The experiences I had there are unequalled. The birds, the people, the land all changed me, but I missed Ty every day. Everything smelled wrong and tasted different. And I never got what I ordered in restaurants because no one could understand me. I just felt so alone. I dreamt one night that I heard a tapping at my window and found Ty there, having flown across the ocean, fighting his way past cockatoos to find me and take away my homesickness. I only missed him more.

The night I came home from Australia, I didn't go home. The first place I went was The Ranch, desperate to see Ty and afraid that he would be uninterested in my return. I had been told that in my absence he had made many friends, learned to do a spot-on imitation of a white-faced whistling tree duck—he was basically the belle of the ball. So I opened the door and turned on the light to the room he was in with little expectation.

"Hi, Ty," I said cautiously.

He blinked his eyes, silent, staring. Then he bobbed his head, regurgitating whatever he could find in his crop to feed me with. I was hardly forgotten, merely displaced.

In my current job(s) it isn't unusual for me to be on the road. That trip to Australia changed the way I feel about travelling, though, and especially about coming home. Sometimes I swear I see Booth, my Brittany Spaniel from the corner of my eye, curled at my feet. I hear Ty in the voice of children scampering through the hotel hallway. In quiet moments on the road, I think I am home. Ty has taught me to take him with me and all the things I love. He has taught me to be confident that all I have left will be waiting right where I left it when I come home. Home is always waiting. The relationship you build training your parrot can last a lifetime!

7

Vocal Behaviors

Everybody loves a talking parrot. You have probably seen talking parrots doing routines in bird shows at zoos and in videos on the Internet. Maybe you have even wondered how these routines were trained. It was seeing Alex, the famous African grey parrot, being trained an episode of *Nature* titled "Look Who's Talking" that made me decide I wanted to be a bird trainer. I had always loved birds and had them in my life, but seeing that program cinched it for me. Years later I couldn't help but feel that my life had come full circle when the follow-up episode of *Nature* titled "Extraordinary Birds" included me and an African grey parrot named Quasar doing a show at Disney's Animal Kingdom. So as you can imagine I have a soft spot for birds that talk and do vocal routines.

If you have a parrot who readily talks, training him to offer vocal behaviors on cue is actually rather simple. It just takes a little time and repetition. Most of our other pets do not use words, and this makes parrots seem closer to us. There even are parrots that know how to use words appropriately in context. It is easy to laugh and hard to be lonely when there is a parrot in your home that sounds just like you. And if you spend time training your parrot to offer vocal behaviors on cue with positive reinforcement, your parrot is likely to offer up even more words and sounds!

If having a parrot who talks is important to you, consider adopting one who is known to be a talker.

If You Teach Your Bird to Whistle, Will He Still Learn to Talk?

One of the more common myths about teaching your parrot to talk is that if he learns to whistle first he will be less likely to learn to speak. Supposedly this is because talking is harder than whistling. That isn't really true. Parrots make a wide variety of noises and mimic a lot more than words. They are likely to whistle, beep, and ring as well as talk. It may be that whistling is less difficult to learn, but learning to whistle won't stop a parrot from talking. Some parrots may enjoy whistling and never learn to talk, but this is an individual preference, not a generality. Remember that while it is enjoyable for a parrot to learn all kinds of noises, the main reason for mimicking is for interaction. The more attention a bird gets for making a particular sound, the more likely he is to repeat it. So if you want your bird to talk, you may not want to respond to your bird when he whistles and instead pay attention to other noises or anything that sounds as if it might become talking.

Will my Parrot Talk?

There is no guarantee that a parrot that comes into your home will talk. Every bird is an individual, and even a species that is known for its talking ability may not ever say a word.

The Parrot's Background

If having a parrot who talks is very important to you, consider finding a bird that needs rehoming and already talks. He still may not learn a bunch of new words and phrases, but he is likely to continue to say the things he has learned once he's comfortable in your home. Also he is more likely to pick up new words than a parrot that has never talked. There are thousands of parrots out there in need of a loving home. You would be making a tremendous difference in that parrot's life.

Parrots learn to imitate sounds as a way to interact with their environment and the other animals (including humans) in it. Don't worry too much about having to raise a parrot from a baby in order to get him to talk. Even a parrot that needs work being socialized and learning to step up can be a talker. While it certainly may be easier to work with a hand-raised bird, being raised by hand does not necessarily make him more likely to speak. There are parrots that were taken from the wild and never tamed that talk, although their tendency is to learn to say very little. Even if your parrot was not hand-raised, if you spend time with him, handle him, and interact with him frequently; he is likely to learn some vocalizations to get your attention. Parrots are social animals, so interacting with their environment is very rewarding to them. No matter how your parrot was raised, he may still learn to talk.

The Parrot's Species

There are certain species that are more likely to mimic human speech. Surprisingly, one of the species is the budgerigar. Little budgies (usually called parakeets in the United States) can learn a surprising number of words. In fact, these exuberant little guys are a blast to train to do tricks as well. African greys and Amazon parrots are also renowned for their potential for speaking abilities. Amazons especially seem to love to sing. Of course there are many other species such as macaws and cockatoos that talk as well. Some of the little

African greys, budgies and Amazons are three of the parrots that are most likely to talk.

parrots, including cockatiels and those in the genera *Pionus* and *Poicephalus*, will also pick up a few words. Just remember if you are choosing a parrot to bring into your home that there is no guarantee of talking ability. Be sure you pick your parrot based on a variety of reasons that make the species or the individual bird irresistible to you.

The Parrot's Age

While you may be anxious for your young parrot to start talking, be patient. You may hear of parrots coming into a home at an age of three months and already talking. This does happen sometimes, but for the most part parrots do not start talking until they are a year or even two years old. It often happen that after that first word is said the flood gates open and the words come rushing out. If you have an adult bird that has been rehomed, be patient as well. It often takes months or even a year before a parrot acclimates, gets into the routine of the household, and offers up a few words. There are some things you can do, however, to encourage your parrot to speak up.

Encouraging Vocal Behaviors

Surprisingly, parrots achieve speech without the vocal folds (cords) that humans use and without the assistance of lips. Just try to say "apple" without using your lips and you'll realize that parrots must use a very different process from the one humans use to produce sounds. Dr. Irene Pepperberg did a bit of work on figuring this out with her African grey parrot Alex. African grey parrots likely use their esophagus, trachea, and glottis to create pressure build-ups and bursts that mimic the bursts created by our lips. Parrots also use tongue placement and the amount the beak is open to manipulate sound. That they use different anatomy to produce words is interesting, but the question on everyone's mind is "*Why* do parrots talk?"

No one is sure why parrots talk in our homes. There is a lot more research to be done on parrot communication in wild flocks. That it is a bit of mystery perhaps makes it all the more fascinating and fun when our parrots speak. Although scientists agree that parrots do not use language in the complex way that we do, Alex proved to the world that parrots can indeed use words to label objects and actions, leaving us to wonder how much our parrots are really saying.

Talking to your parrot is one of the best ways to encourage him to talk.

The first step in teaching a vocal behavior is figuring out what you would like your bird to say. Keep it clean and don't choose something meant to make another household member angry. You all have to live together! And if something happens to you, your parrot may need to live in a new home. Pick something that is fun, that will make you smile, and that you will not mind hearing often.

Talk to Your Parrot

This seems like the most obvious way to get your parrot to talk, and it is probably the most important thing you can do to nurture a talking parrot. Fill his world with words. If you live by yourself, this is permission to talk to yourself. If you are going to have an animated conversation on the phone, have it near the parrot. The more your parrot hears the more he is likely to pick up, especially if you are talking to him.

Make sure that you stop and talk to your parrot. Most of us do this, of course. We talk to our parrots all the time to say hello, ask them how they are doing, give them their breakfast, and ask them whether they want to come out. All of these things are some of the most common things parrots learn to say. So if you want a talking parrot, don't be embarrassed—talk to him!

Learn to Learn

A parrot familiar with training for fun and interaction is a better candidate for learning new things than a parrot that has never learned that offering behavior when asked might get him a reward. So if you want your parrot to say a few more things, it is a good idea to start by training some simple behaviors. Teaching a bird to wave, turn, or target can be fun and less frustrating that something more difficult such as offering vocal behavior. However, a parrot that has "learned to learn" and has been rewarded for this with attention and treats will be more likely to use his creativity to try and figure out what you are asking. The same is true with learning to repeat a word or, if your parrot does not talk, a whistle or other noise. After your parrot has done it once, it will be easier to repeat the process.

Another way to encourage your parrot to talk is to reward him for making new sounds.

Pay Attention

Remember that a behavior repeats itself only if it has been reinforced. If you want your parrot to offer new behaviors, reinforce him for them. When you see your parrot do something that is new, stop to visit with him. Give him a treat. If your parrot gets your attention for doing new and interesting

Talking in Multiple Parrot Households

Many people think that the only way a parrot will talk is if he lives alone. This is perhaps most frequently said of parakeets, because when two birds are together in the same cage they often do not talk. This is not because they won't talk, however. If your parrot comes out of the cage and frequently spends time with you, then having multiple parrots in the house can sometimes make all the birds in the house more likely to talk. Parrots often learn behaviors from one another, including talking. If one of your parrots is a blabbermouth when he interacts with you, the other parrots in the house might pick up a few words from him.

things, he will get creative and continue to offer new things. This is true of sounds as well. Even if your parrot is not saying anything, he is likely offering whistles and maybe even household noises like the sound of the phone or the microwave. When you hear your parrot make a new sound, make a big deal out of it. He will start offering up new noises to get your attention once more.

Don't worry too much about the fact that you are encouraging your parrot to make noises or to whistle when he is not yet talking. Many people think that if a parrot learns to whistle he will be less likely to learn to talk. In my experience this is not true. There are parrots that whistle and do not talk, but most parrots that talk also whistle. So there is not necessarily a correlation between whistling and not learning to talk. Bird trainer Barbara Heidenreich did a survey of more than 900 parrot owners with talking birds and found that more than 70 percent of the parrots that talked also whistled. So just focus on encouraging your bird to offer as many sounds as possible.

Say it Often

Parrots do sometimes learn to say a word that they have heard only a couple of times, but the vast majority of things they say they have heard many times. This is especially true of a parrot that is new to talking. You may even hear your parrot practicing sounds that are soon to be a word. It may take some time to work out how to say the word correctly. For this a parrot sometimes needs to hear a word many times. So say the words you want your parrot to learn frequently. You can even make a recording of what you want your parrot to learn to say and loop it so that it plays while you are gone. There are also some CDs available of words and sounds to teach your parrot to mimic. Playing a CD for your parrot is another great way to give him the opportunity to hear sounds repeatedly. There is no guarantee he will pick these words up, but you will at least increase the possibility.

Give it Context

Another way to get a bird to learn a particular word is to give it context. If the word you want your bird to learn is "apple," then say "apple" every time you give him a slice. Use the name of every food you offer. Say "breakfast" when you put

Using a word in context—such as saying "apple" when you give your bird an apple—can help your parrot learn to say that word.

his food bowl into his cage in the morning. Say "Do you want to go back?" when you put your parrot away at night. Use the same phrase or word for all the normal events of a day as well. Some parrots are more likely to say a word if it is a label for something. The great thing about putting words in context is that it also gives your parrot a way to communicate with you. When my African grey parrot Ty says "good night" he means that he thinks it is time for me to turn off the lights. In fact, he won't stop saying it until I do. Even a parrot likes to get a good night's sleep!

You can also go a step further and make the word you are trying to teach more interesting by being animated. If the word "apple" is said with gusto and followed by a scene this too might it a more appealing sound to repeat. (Go ahead, dance and cheer. No one is looking!) Make learning to speak fun and your parrot may be more likely to pick up a few words.

Capturing Vocal Behaviors

Once your parrot is saying on cue something that you want to get, it is time to capture the behavior. We have discussed a few instances in capturing behaviors in the previous chapters. Capturing, remember, is catching your parrot in the act of doing something you want to get when you give him a cue and then

Do Parrots Understand What They Are Saying?

Parrots have an uncanny ability to say the right thing at the right time. Dr. Irene Pepperberg's 30 years of work with Alex, an African grey parrot, demonstrated that parrots can certainly label items in their world, using the correct word for the correct item. Alex could identify 50 objects; he could also name their colors, shapes, and the materials they were made from. He also understood the concepts of bigger, smaller, same, and different. The parrot in your home may learn to use the right word for many things and may even utter phrases at the appropriate moment, but he won't learn language the way humans use it. Your parrot may say, "Goodbye, I'll see you tonight," when you leave because that is the appropriate sound for when you pick up your keys and head for the door. He doesn't really know that "see you tonight" means you'll be back around 6 pm.

rewarding him for giving it to you. Most of the behaviors we have looked at training involve shaping. With getting a sound or word on cue, you start by simply rewarding the vocalization when you hear it.

Start by training one word at a time. If you reward for multiple sounds you will confuse your poor parrot, who may not understand quite why he is getting treats and attention. If you reward just one vocalization until it is solidly on cue, your parrot will be very clear on what you are after. This will be important when you transition from rewarding the word every time it is offered to rewarding only when it is offered after the cue. To start, though, pick one word and reward it every time you hear it.

Many parrots will not say new words when someone is in the room. You may need to hide around a corner to catch your bird saying whatever you are trying to train him to say.

Say it Again

When you are trying to capture a vocal behavior, your event marker is the best tool in your box. Chances are that you will not be standing right in front of your parrot's cage when he says the word you are trying to capture. This is not a problem if you use your event marker. Even if you are on the other side of the house when you hear your parrot say the word, you can shout out "good" and come running with a treat. Sometimes the challenge involved with rewarding your parrot, though, is just trying to get him to offer the behavior.

Many parrots will not say new words, and some will not talk at all when someone is in the room. A great way to get your parrot to offer the behavior is to leave the room. Pick a time of the day when your parrot is normally chattering and walk out of sight to give your bird a chance to chatter. Hide around the corner and listen if your parrot talks softly. Be careful not to startle your parrot when he says what you are looking for, but call out "good" and bring him a treat or give him a scratch on the head.

Some parrots are also more likely to talk during certain household events or noises. Running water, vacuuming, or maybe your afternoon workout to your favorite exercise CD might get your parrot to start chattering. Some parrots like it when you turn up the tunes; this gets them to start singing and talking. Start paying attention to when your parrot offers up the most vocalization and use this to your advantage. Turn on the kitchen faucet and do some dishes while you wait for your parrot to say "hello" or whatever you are trying to capture.

Capture it

Let's say you are training your parrot to say "hello." The first couple of times you reward your parrot for saying "hello" he may not quite understand what is going on. It will not take him long to figure it out. As soon as he figures out he is getting attention and treats for saying "hello" he will call for you every time he wants to get you to come over and spend some time with him. When he is offering "hello" frequently, you can start being picky about what you reward.

Make sure that you are rewarding the exact "hello" that you want. This is the

Choosing a Cue

Be sure to give careful consideration to what you use for a cue for vocal behaviors. You want your cue to be short, versatile, and easy to remember. To avoid confusion, it should also sound different from any other cue you are using. Give some thought to the fact you will say this word and likely hear this word often as well. Chances are that your parrot will quickly learn to say the cue along with the word. This can be very amusing to listen to as long as the cue is not something annoying or offensive.

When your parrot is repeating the desired word frequently, start rewarding him only when he says it on cue.

time to make sure you reward him only when he says the word clearly. If there is a particular way that he says it that you enjoy—perhaps he elongates the o—you can choose to reward only when he says it in that particular way. Take care not to frustrate him. If he says "hello" six or seven times the wrong way and hasn't been rewarded, go back to rewarding him. He does not quite understand he is being rewarded for saying it a particular way. Then try again to reward only the preferred behavior. Then once he is offering the word clearly and the way you want it, it is time to get it on cue.

Getting it on Cue

Switching from rewarding your parrot for offering the vocal behavior to getting it on cue is tricky. Your parrot has gotten used to being rewarded for just offering the behavior; he may get frustrated with no longer getting an automatic treat.

This will be especially challenging the first time. However, the more you train vocal behaviors, the more likely your parrot will make this transition quickly. So if you struggle with this the first time, know that it will get easier.

Starting Out

At this stage your parrot will likely be saying "hello" over and over again. Start offering your cue. Let's say that your cue is "Say 'hi.'" Start giving this cue frequently when your parrot is already talking. When there is a silence, say the cue and then wait six seconds. If he doesn't say "hello," repeat the cue. When your parrot accidentally says "hello" after the cue, mark the event and reward him. Try to catch him a few times, and do not reward him when he says "hello" if you have not offered the cue.

To train for an immediate response, be careful to only reward your parrot when he says "hello" within two seconds of you giving him the cue.

Your parrot may get frustrated and not understand that you are rewarding him only for offering his behavior after the cue. If he stops offering "hello" when you are trying to cue him, end the session. Then take a step back in training. Reward him a couple of times when hear him saying "hello." When he is in a talking mood, try again to get him to offer the behavior no more than six seconds after the cue, and don't reward him when he says it at other times.

You may find when you are trying to get "hello" on cue that your parrot offers it at first only when you are out of the room. It can get a little time consuming, but leave the room and wait for your parrot to start talking. Or just move out of sight and work on other things while you wait for your parrot get starting saying "hello" again. Then when he is starting to offer it, call out the cue and see whether you can get him to offer "hello" right after you give him the "Say hi" cue. I have found that it is frequently easier to get a parrot started when I am not standing in front of his cage.

Training for an Immediate Response

It will take a few sessions before your parrot is consistently offering a vocal behavior on cue. When you are certain your parrot understands he is being rewarded for saying "hello" only following the cue, get a little tougher with your

Does It Matter Whether My Parrot is Male or Female?

It is true that in some species males are more likely to have a larger repertoire of sounds and words. This is particularly true in cockatiels and parakeets, but there are often exceptions to this. The better likelihood of males learning to talk may have something to do with their natural behavior in the wild, where perhaps the male is more vocal. However, the females have all the right parts and the ability, just maybe not the propensity. In most parrots, like macaws, Amazons, and African greys, the sex of the bird makes no difference in whether or not the bird speaks. Males and females are just as able and just as likely (or unlikely) to learn to talk. Whether or not a parrot learns is all about the individual. Some parrots are just natural-born talkers and some are not.

If you record your parrot's sounds and words, you can use the recordings to try to get him to repeat them later.

expectations. Do not reward him if it takes several seconds to offer the behavior. Cue him and give two seconds; cue him again and if in two seconds you do not get the appropriate response, turn your back. You may even walk away. This is how you train immediate response. If you cue him repeatedly and reward him no matter long it takes to offer the vocal behavior, you are training latency and sloppy behavior.

Be Precise

Take care with your event marker when you are training vocal behaviors as well. If you interrupt your parrot when he is saying "hello" to say "good" and hand him a treat, you can easily shorten the behavior. This goes for offering attention as well. If you come running into the room before your parrot has completed the vocal behavior, you are jumping the gun on the reward. Wait until your parrot has said the whole word or completed the entire sound and them mark the event and offer a treat or make a big deal out it.

Lost Words

The only problem with using capturing as a method of training is that if something happens to extinguish the behavior—meaning your parrot no longer says the word or makes the sound—you have to start from scratch. And if your parrot stops making a sound that you cannot mimic, you may never be able to get your parrot to repeat it again. If you do have a word that your parrot stops saying that you want to get back on cue again, just start over by saying the word until you can get your parrot to repeat it. You may be able to get it back on cue quickly, but you have to begin as if it were a new behavior. If you have a sound on cue that you really love and cannot make yourself, it is a good idea to record it. That way if your parrot stops making the sound you can play the recording to try to get him going again.

Creating a Talking Routine

You can have a lot of fun with a parrot that knows how to say a word or two on cue. In fact, one of my favorite routines with a talking parrot only requires that the parrot say the word "four" on cue. The response has to be immediate and the behavior well trained for this routine to work, but it is a real crowd pleaser. The "four" routine is a great first vocal routine.

Training the "Four" Routine—A Math Competition

Props Needed: None

Cue: Verbal cue of "three"

Desired Behavior: When you say "three" the parrot says "four."

Steps:

1. Parrot begins to say "four".
2. Says "four" frequently.
3. Says "four" clearly.
4. Says "four" when you say "three".
5. Says "four" immediately after you say "three".

Directions

Start by training your parrot to say "four." Say the word often or get a recording and play it for your bird. If your parrot is not learning to say it, try saying it during playtime and saying it with enthusiasm. Once you hear your parrot starting to say "four," give him attention for it. You do not want to begin fully marking the event and rewarding him, because you want him to continue working on learning to say the word until he is saying it perfectly. A little encouragement goes a long way, though!

My Parrot Won't Talk

So you were hoping for a talking parrot, and yours has yet to say a word. What do you do? First of all, accept your parrot for the wonderful pet that he already is. Talking will not change your parrot's personality, so focus on the things you love about your parrot. Some of the greatest parrots in the world have never spoken a word but communicate just fine. Talking is not the mark of a great parrot. You can still get other vocal behaviors on cue such as beeps and whistles. You can still have tons of fun with your bird!

When your parrot is saying "four" well, begin to mark the event and reward him whenever he says it. Soon he will be offering the word all the time. When he is saying it frequently, you can get a little bit picky about when your reward it. Do not tell him "good" and bring him a treat unless he says "four" with clarity and does not truncate the word or say it too quickly. You want to start reinforcing only perfect "fours" so that your parrot is very clear about what you are asking. Reward sloppy words and that is what he will offer.

Once your parrot is offering up the perfect "four" with maddening frequency, you can start working on getting it on cue. While he's on a talking jag, say the word "three." Say it several times, waiting a few seconds in between to try and catch your parrot saying "four" directly after. If he says "four" after you say "three," mark the event and reward him. Do not reward him unless he offers the word after the cue, but give him five seconds or so to offer it. Once he seems to understand the cue, you can then reward him only when he says "four" immediately after the cue.

Now that he understands the cue, you can start working on the routine. If he knows other words on cue, mix it up and ask him a few different things to make sure he understands that "three" is the cue for "four." This may take a few sessions; if he gets lost, back up and focus on "four" again. Now you are ready to do some math!

Next is to get your parrot to understand that the cue may come at the end of a sentence and he has to listen for it. Try asking him questions that end in "three" and mark the event and reward him if he says four. If he is confused try asking him just the cue a couple of times, then add in the sentences again. The lines to the four routine are:

- What is 7 minus 3?
- What is 1 plus 3?
- What is 12 divided by 3?
- What is the square root of 49 minus 3?

You can ask these questions either to show off your parrot's supposed math skills or to have a math competition. This works best with kids who have to think a little to get the answer. When you ask, "What's 12 divided by 3" the kid will be thinking while your parrot blurts out "four" because he doesn't have to mull over the answer. He will just respond to the cue. Your parrot will look like a math genius!

Multiple Word Routines

Once you have gotten several vocal behaviors on cue, you may want to put together a routine just for the fun of it. You have probably seen videos of parrots that offer a variety of sounds on cue, and maybe you've wondered how the trainer does it. Each sound is cued by a single word or short phrase. Some of the more complicated-sounding routines are just filled with a smattering of quick cues that the parrot has learned to listen

When training a vocal routine, reward your parrot when he speaks clearly so he will be easy for others to understand.

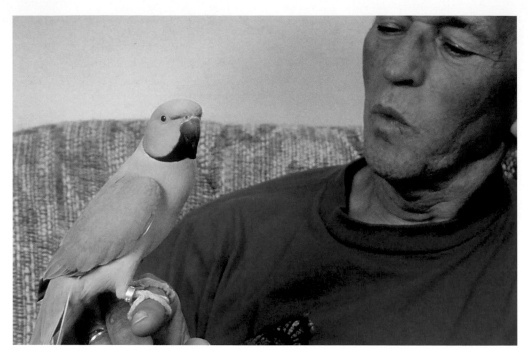

Once you have gotten several vocal behaviors on cue, you can put them together into a routine.

for and respond to appropriately. Maybe the cue for the parrot to laugh is "joke" and the trainer says, "So did you hear the one about the parrot that had to go into therapy? He wanted more out of life than a cracker but just didn't know how to say it... Isn't that a great joke?" The parrot hears "joke" and laughs. Later in the routine the trainer might say, "So my boyfriend took me to Taco Bell for our anniversary dinner. What a joke." Again the parrot laughs. If you have solidly trained cues and can come up with a bit of inventive dialogue this can be a lot of fun.

A Cue for Each Behavior

The first step in getting your parrot to offer multiple vocal behaviors on cue is to make sure your parrot understands that each behavior has a distinct cue. When a parrot first learns to say a few things when asked, he will likely generalize. He can tell by the tone of your voice and body language that you are asking for a vocal behavior. So he may just run through them all until he hits the right one. When he is first learning, it is okay to let him do that. Give him a chance to understand that each cue is specific to a particular sound.

Once he obviously understands that each word has an individual cue, you need to make your criteria stricter. Cue him and walk away if you get the wrong response. Do not reward him if he offers you the correct behavior second or third, only if it is the first behavior he gives you. You can come back and try again in a moment, but this way you are making it clear that he gets only one chance to give you the right word. Your routine won't work if he just offers a string of vocal behaviors before giving you the right one.

Building up to Sentences

Next you can begin to ask your parrot questions and say sentences that end with the cues you have taught him. For example, "Check out the pretty lady in the front row. Can you say hi?" Then pause and give your parrot a chance to respond to the cue "say hi" with, "hello." If your parrot does not understand, ask him the cue separately and when he offers it, mark the event, reward, and then try it again at the end of a phrase. Your parrot should pick up on this quickly. Then try to get

Modeling

Parrots are flock animals, and in the wild they often model the behaviors of their flock mates and learn from one another. This holds true even in your home. If you have multiple parrots with a propensity to talk or mimic noises, chances are that all your parrots are going to learn the same words. I have heard most of a flock of parrots in an aviary learn to say "hello" just because one parrot was introduced that knew the word. They did not interact a lot with people, but they enjoyed saying "hello" to one another all the same. So if you have multiple parrots in your home, try training the parrot that learns to talk the fastest the desired vocal behavior first. The rest of the parrots are likely to follow suit!

Parrots are more likely to learn words that are said with emotion or emphasis. If you are not careful, you could end up with a foul-mouthed bird!

him to offer a couple of behaviors this way. Also, keep in mind that things will be even easier for your parrot if you have a routine in which the words and sounds are in the same order every time.

When you first start working on the behavior, reward your parrot after each vocal behavior. Keep the treats small so that it doesn't take that long for him to finish them. Then watch until he is no longer nibbling and you have his attention before you ask for the next word. Once you have put together a routine that your parrot pretty much has down, you can reward him after every two or three behaviors. Or if it is a short routine, wait to reward him at the end.

Hopefully you have some great ideas for things to train your parrot to say that will make living with your parrot a joy. Living with a talking parrot can be a great deal of fun. However, there can be a dark side to parrots that talk if they learn to say the wrong things.

Discouraging Unwanted Speech

It seems that everyone has a story about a parrot that curses. In fact most of the tales of parrots in history include that the parrot has a foul mouth that got it into trouble at some point. While there certainly are parrots who curse, it isn't that cursing is a favorite parrot pastime; it's that people seem to love the idea of it. It is true that parrots are more likely to learn words and phrases that are said with some oomph. After all, if someone is screaming it, it must be fun. Yet you could yell out just about anything and the parrot is a little more likely to learn it. Parrots often learn to call the dog or yell for a teenager to come to the phone. So if you don't want your parrot to curse, it's probably a good idea to be careful what you say the next time you stub your toe.

Summing Up

One of the best things about training vocal behaviors with your parrot is that your bird gets in tune with what noises and sounds get your attention. Even better, you get practice in the habit of rewarding the noises you would rather hear than screaming. Talking and flying are two of the things that people admire most in parrots as pets, although keeping flying parrots can be a controversial topic. In the next chapter we will look at training a parrot that is flighted.

Oh, Crack!

Your mom told you this and maybe you didn't listen: "Be careful what you say." The things you say in private, the naughty things that could offend or create gossip, these things slip out in unwanted circumstances when you've had enough practice on the sly.

I know.

I worked at Disney's Animal Kingdom for several years. Everything I said on stage was scrutinized for double entendre and intent. Sometimes I slipped up. If in your personal life everything that excites you is punctuated with the "f" word, it will slip out when you're on the stage, trust me. And even if you stop at "Wasn't that f- I mean, awesome?" children will giggle, adults will complain, and you *might* keep your job.

Got a potty mouth you need to keep in check? Watch out with a parrot. Even if you think you have a perfect vocabulary, you're walking a fine line. When a stubbed toe causes you to exclaim "fudge" and something amazing makes you yell, "Shut the front door!" the parrot is still listening. He'll make it sound dirtier than the real thing.

So the day I sat yawning in front of the television, looked up at the time (I was *so* going to be late to work) and Ty gasped "Oh, crack!" I was sure it was the dirtiest thing I had ever heard. And to make it worse, I laughed until I cried. And *oh, crap*, I was late to work anyway.

So I have a kindergarten teacher's mouth most of the time now, but keeping it clean wasn't really what I learned from Ty. If I listened well, I heard my state of mind. Parrots are wonderful at imitating our words if they are particularly emotive. So if everything was "oh, crack!", "criminy," and "for the love of Bob," then something had to give. When all I heard was cleaned-up exasperation, I started wondering why I wasn't happy.

So these days I listen. And I love it when I hear, "That is so cool!" and lots of laughter coming from the parrot. I know I'm doing a good job being me, even if—oh, crack!—as usual, I'm late. Your parrot can be the voice of the house. Encourage him!

8

Training Free-Flighted Parrots

have lived with free-flighted birds throughout most of my adult life. All of my falconry birds have been released to the sky on a nearly daily basis during the hunting season. One of my favorite things in the world is watching my flock of pigeons circling above me while I sip my morning coffee. And all of the years I spent training birds in a show situation involved a tremendous number of free-flight birds in a variety of situations. Yet despite all of this I am squeamish about the idea of my personal parrots flying free, not just outside, but even in the house in case they still might get outside. I could not explain to you where my double standard comes from exactly, but I can say with certainty that whether or not you clip your parrot's wings is a personal decision that you should make for yourself.

Should I Let My Parrot Fly?

In many countries other than the United States, the prevailing attitude is that clipping a bird's wings is tantamount to cruelty. There are many who argue that birds were meant to fly and that we have no right to take that away from them. In

There is no right or wrong answer to the question of whether or not you should clip your parrot's wings.

the United States, however, the attitude for years has been that the only way to truly ensure a parrot's safety is to keep him from flying. Both of these attitudes have some truth to them.

Reasons to Clip

There are many dangers in our households for a parrot. A parrot that can fly might find himself flying into a ceiling fan or a pot of boiling water. If a parrot on the wing falls into the toilet or the bath, he could drown quickly. A brazen flighted parrot might fly right up to a dog and become a snack. Then there is the trouble that can occur if a door or window is left open. A parrot with limited flight skills that finds itself outdoors may be in a world of trouble. Every day there are announcements of missing parrots that have found their way outside. So it stands to reason that clipping a parrot's wings can eliminate a lot of these risks and keep your beloved bird safe.

Adding Flight to Tricks

If your parrot is flighted and you have trained him to recall and to station, you can add flight into the tricks you are training. Retrieves can easily involve flight. You can have your parrot fly somewhere to retrieve a ball and then fly back to put it into the basket. You can also use your target training to get your parrot to fly to the destination where you want him to climb, slide, or burrow. If you have a parrot that is confident with flying, give him some constructive ways to burn off energy and use his wings.

Reasons not to Clip

The flip side of this is the effects of being clipped can have on a parrot's well-being. Many parrots that have been clipped are clumsy and unsure of themselves physically. This equates to timid and fearful behavior and a parrot who is not at ease with the world. Sometimes clumsiness is just about a bad wing clip, but there are some parrots that are just unsteady no matter how they are clipped. Then there is also the question of how much potential confidence is lost when a parrot cannot maneuver and explore his territory the way he could on the wing. Overall, there is the possibility a parrot with clipped wings might not be as well adjusted as a bird that is allowed to fly.

Distractions

Whenever you are training something new or training in a new place, keep in mind the variety of distractions that can slow down your training session. Many a well-trained parrot has been struck dumb when brought onto a television sound stage. Bright lights, camera close-ups, a large audience, and other strangeness can be overwhelmingly distracting. That is why many a parrot has choked when he had a big moment for potential fame. In smaller ways we face these challenges in our home. Keep in mind that the dog wandering into the room, the house being demolished across the street, and even that new lamp you bought for the living room can be a distraction that brings your training to a halt. Try to keep distractions to a minimum if you are training something new.

Small birds that are clipped and larger birds that are growing out of a clip may actually be able to fly well enough to escape. If something startles your parrot and a door or window is open, he may fly right through and into the wild. Once outside your parrot may fly some ways away. Unfortunately, a parrot that is clipped and not used to flying will not have the skills to maneuver. He may not know how to fly down to you, which takes some practice. A bird that is outside and not a good flyer may not only end up far away but also could easily become prey to a savvy predator. Some proponents of flight training point to this scenario as a reason to allow your parrot to learn how to fly before preventing it from flying by clipping the parrot's wings.

I have not seen any research to support the theory that parrots who can fly are healthier than those that cannot. However, I have talked to veterinarians who postulate this may be likely. A parrot's circulatory system and heart as well as skeletal and muscular system are designed specifically to support flight. It is possible that the lack of flight can have an adverse effect on a parrot's health. Flight certainly is an excellent form of exercise for parrots, and an obese bird will have health problems.

Leaving your parrot flighted makes it more difficult to keep him safe, but it has physical and possibly psychological benefits for the bird.

It's Your Decision

So in the end, you must weigh the pros and cons for yourself and make your own decision. Educate yourself on all of the pitfalls of either side of the argument and make sure you are prepared to do the best you can for your parrot. If you have multiple parrots you may decide that one bird would be better off fully flighted and another should remained clipped. It is your home, your parrot is your responsibility, and you have to make decisions with which you are the most comfortable.

Flight Training at Fledging Age

There are many experts who suggest that all parrots should be given an opportunity to learn to fly before their wings are clipped. Anecdotally, people note parrots that have learned to use their wings have a lot more coordination.

Many experts suggest letting a parrot learn to fly even if you intend to clip his wings. This seems especially beneficial for African greys.

Proponents of fledging their parrots before clipping feel that these parrots are not as likely to fall off perches or land badly once they are clipped.

It has been noted that African grey parrots especially benefit from learning to fly. Their heavy-breasted build can make them particularly clumsy when clipped. I am not sure whether this is true, but I did let my African grey fledge before I clipped him, and he is not a clumsy bird. All the same, I spoke to a very conscientious parrot owner recently who let her young African grey fledge. The parrot had been flying for only a week when she escaped out a briefly opened door and six months later still had not been found. Even letting your parrot fly briefly is something you should decide on carefully.

So if you have a young parrot that you think you would like to keep fully flighted, make sure to give him opportunities to learn to fly when he is young. While a parrot can learn to fly when he is older, it is a lot more challenging. In those first few weeks and months when his primary and secondary feathers have just grown in he is ready to learn and quickly absorb lessons. He has had no negative experiences with flying and therefore a lot less reluctance to try new things on the wing. A parrot that has had a lot of negative experiences with attempting to fly because his wings have been clipped will be much more reluctant to learn. So if you have the opportunity, let a young parrot spread his wings.

If you have an outdoor aviary where he can practice, this is ideal. You want to give your parrot an opportunity to learn not only how to fly from one point to another but also how to fly down and maneuver in a variety of ways on the wing. You can work on these skills in your home, but there are more obstacles and potential trouble inside your house than there would be in an aviary. Once your parrot begins to get on the wing, you should start your training immediately. A flighted bird is actually quite manageable in your home if he will consistently recall on cue.

Recall

Recall is the ability to get a parrot to come to you when you call him. Having a solid recall is critical to remaining sane in a home with a flighted parrot. A parrot

Comfort Level

With a parrot that is learning to recall or building flight skills, it is important to pay attention to his comfort level. Flying can be terrifying for a parrot that has not had much experience. When stopping often means crashing and getting down from a high place is a mystery, this is completely understandable. As with the other behaviors described in this book, let your parrot go at his own pace and be in control of the situation. If you are determined to teach him to fly, you may be in it for the long haul. Be patient. Be kind. Let your parrot take each step when he is ready and do everything you can to help him succeed. It is very important not to push him past his comfort level.

One of the early steps of training the recall is to have your parrot hop a short distance to your hand.

that can fly can easily get to places you cannot reach without a ladder. That can be a problem if you do not want your parrot on top of the china cabinet or need to put him into his cage. The secret to having a parrot that comes when he is called is training, repetition, and positive reinforcement.

Training and repetition will help your parrot understand what it is that you want him to do. It is the positive reinforcement, however, that will convince your parrot that it is worth his while to come to you. This is a perfect example of why positive reinforcement is the best choice when training a bird. A flighted bird has a tremendous amount of control over where he chooses to go, and if coming to you has any negative connotation he may choose not to come. Having spent years depending on my training to call a falcon down from 1,000 feet above me with nothing more than a bit of food and a long history of positive reinforcement, I feel confident that you can train your parrot to come down to you from the top of your bookshelf. And when he does, it will be an amazing feeling.

Props Needed: None

Cue: Verbal cue of "Come on" and physical cue of holding out perch hand.

Desired Behavior: Parrot comes to you, lands on your outstretched hand, and stays when you present your hand and call for him to "Come on".

Steps:

- Parrot targets to you.
- Targets to you from a foot away.
- Parrot steps up.
- Stretches leg to step up.
- Uses beak while stretching to get onto hand.
- Parrot hops to the hand.
- Hops and flaps to the hand.
- Flaps a couple of wing beats in order to get to the hand.
- Flies two feet to hand.
- Flies four feet to hand.

Instructions

If your parrot has been clipped and never learned to fly, this training may take some time. Imagine if you were learning to ride a unicycle after an abandoned effort as a child. All you would remember is that it was hard and you fell down a lot. You would be slow to learn again as an adult after all this negative experience. It is similar with a parrot that has been clipped and has plenty of experience crashing. This training may go very slowly, especially with the bigger parrots. Smaller parrots, however, which have more lift and ability even when they are clipped, may take to flying right away. Just be patient with your parrot. It will be worth the effort!

Start With the Step Up

It is important that your parrot has a very solid "Step up" response and plenty of history being on your hand and stepping up before you get to the recall. If you have a parrot that is hand shy, you are going to need to take the time to work on

Your ultimate goal is to have your parrot fly to your hand whenever you give the "come on" cue.

getting him comfortable with stepping up. Provide him with some experience getting treats and having fun hanging out with you. The more confident your parrot is with stepping up to you and walking around on your hand, the more likely you are going to be able get him to make the leap to flying to you.

Start your recall process by getting your parrot to target to your hand and step up. Then have him target to your hand from a short distance before stepping up. Say "Come on," mark the event when he steps on your hand, and reward her. If you are working in an aviary, get him to walk down the length of a perch. If you are working inside, have him walk across a table or the counter. This way you are getting him to come to you instead of you coming to him. The next steps will be shaping this behavior to a come to you with a little more effort.

Once your parrot is walking to you and stepping up, position yourself so that your perch hand is just far enough away that your parrot has to stretch a leg to get onto your hand. Approximate until he is stretching as far as he can.

Hop on Up

Then move your hand just far enough away from his perch that he has to hop to get to it. Keep in mind that hopping up is easier than hopping down, so position your hand slightly above his feet and far enough away that he can comfortably make the hop.

Watch your parrot's body language when you get to this point. Is he leaning forward and flapping his wings a little bit? Then he is definitely interested in trying but is just nervous. Give him a couple of chances and then go back to having him come to you with a stretched-out step. If he is interested but reluctant to jump, you can also try to shape the behavior by encouraging wing flaps and any motions that get him close to hopping. Mark the event and reward him, trying to get him to make more of an effort the next time. This can be the hardest step of the training if your parrot is afraid of flying.

If your parrot is sitting tight and not even trying to hop to your hand, he is either not ready to try or losing interest in the training session. Either way, go back to stepping him up and either work on building more confidence or end the

Do a Double Take

Having a parrot flying in your home means a whole new set of dangers of which you should be mindful. Your parrot will have the ability to get out of a dangerous situation more quickly, but he will also have the ability to get into trouble faster than you can see it coming. Every time you let him out of his cage, and especially before you start a training session, do a double take. Look around the house and try to think of every dangerous possibility. We cannot always think of everything, but many accidents can be avoided by at least trying. Here is a short checklist of common household dangers:

- Are windows and door shut?
- Is the ceiling fan turned off?
- Is there anything cooking on the stove?
- Is there anything poisonous or sharp lying about?
- Are other potentially dangerous animals put away?

session. Try to end the session on a positive note, asking him to step up from an easy position so that he can finish up with some success. You may be looking at many training sessions with a parrot that is nervous to use his wings, so keeping it positive and fun is important.

A Little Farther

Once your parrot is hopping to the hand confidently and without hesitating, you can try to get him to hop a little farther, a jump that requires a wing flap for balance. Next, try to get him to make a hop that requires a couple of wing flaps. As long as each step is with confidence, move back a couple of inches more at a time. You will cue him by presenting your perch hand and saying "Come on," mark the event with a "good" or a click when he jumps to your hand, and reward him. Make sure that you do not mark the event until he lands on your hand. The behavior is to land on your hand. If you say "good" when your parrot is halfway to you, then you are marking the halfway point—not what you want. This will be important when he begins to fly to you from greater distances.

Taking Flight

Once your parrot is hopping a couple of feet, it is time to encourage him to fly a short distance to you. Watch your parrot carefully before you cue him. Do not ask him to come until he has finished his treat, is facing you, and you have his attention. One of the most common mistakes trainers make is cuing the parrot when he is not paying attention. This can frustrate you and teach your parrot that you will keep cuing him until he feels like participating. Wait for him to focus on you and cue him only two or three times before dropping your hands for a few moments and then either moving in closer or giving him another chance to fly to you.

As your parrot begins to fly with confidence, you can make your approximations farther, a distance of another couple of feet rather than just a few inches at a time. After all, it is not much harder to fly five feet than three feet. However, what is harder is landing and braking. If your parrot has no experience with this, trust me that it is harder than you might think. He will need practice, and an iffy landing might dent his confidence a little. That's okay; just make things easy for him again.

So as you approximate flying farther distances, if at any time he does not want to come to you, shorten the distance and give him a chance to succeed. Go slowly, making sure not to push him too hard, and give him the opportunity to gain the skill and confidence to fly to you.

Station

Once your parrot has learned the recall and is flying to you with confidence, you may find that your bigger challenge is getting him to stay on the perch until you are ready for him. This is actually good news because it means that he is finding it very reinforcing to come to you. All you have to do is make staying on the perch more reinforcing than flying to you when he is not called.

If your parrot does come to you when you did not call to him, go ahead and hold out your hand for him to land on. You do not want to duck or push him away, which may be unpleasant and give him a reason not to come to you. This is especially true at this stage of training because he probably will not understand why you did not catch him. All he knows is that sometimes you hold out your hand and sometimes you duck, and flying around may be frightening to him. Next time he may not come to you. So go ahead and catch him, but do not say "good" or give him a treat. Don't say anything. Just put him back on the perch and walk away.

Make sure that it is rewarding for your parrot to stay on his station. Otherwise, he may try to fly to you when you don't want him to do so.

After you have trained the flying recall, you can train some tricks that incorporate flying.

It is also a good command for getting your parrot onto the perch. Use the "Step down" that you have trained him and give him a good-sized treat on the perch. You can also do repetitions to the perch where he gets rewarded for stepping down but not for stepping up. Remember that a behavior repeats itself if it is reinforcing, so if you want your parrot to station on his perch and stay until you cue him to come, you have to make it reinforcing to stay on the perch.

When your parrot has the recall completely mastered, you may find that you work a lot on stationing. The way to teach your parrot to come to you only when you call him is to be mindful of what you are rewarding. If he flies to you without being called, do not talk to him and do not let him hang out with you or give him a treat. Do not do anything to make it rewarding, just put him back onto his perch. Then try to catch him with positive reinforcement before he is thinking about flying to you. Remember to stop by and give him attention, a toy to chew on, or a treat when he is staying at his station. Also, ask him to come to you now and then for some attention.

Tricks in Flight

Once you have your parrot doing an in-flight recall with confidence you can train some fun things on the wing. If you have some room to maneuver in your home or an outdoor aviary, you don't have to take your show outside either. Here are a couple of fun things you can train in your home.

Fly Through a Hoop

Props Needed: Hula hoop or some other hoop big enough to fly through, either attached to a stand or held by an assistant.

Cue: Presence of the hoop and presentation of perch hand plus verbal "Come on."

Desired Behavior: Parrot leaves perch, flies through hoop, and lands on trainer's hand.

Steps:

1. Parrot steps up onto trainer's hand through hoop.
2. Hops to trainer's hand through hoop.
3. Flies distance of a foot through hoop to trainer standing in center.
4. Flies several feet through hoop to trainer standing in center.
5. Flies through hoop with trainer standing slightly to the side.
6. Flies through hoop with trainer standing a foot to the side.
7. Flies through hoop with trainer standing several feet to the side.
8. Bends flight through hoop to get to trainer far to the side.

Instructions

Training a parrot to fly through a hoop to come to you is fairly easy if your parrot has mastered the recall. The secret to success is the timing of your event marker. You want your parrot to understand that he is being rewarded for flying through the hoop, not just coming to you. So shaping the behavior involves marking the event appropriately. Throughout the training of flying through the hoop you are going to click or say "good" when your parrot goes through the hoop.

Start by making sure your parrot is not uncomfortable with the hoop. Perhaps leave it in the room where your parrot can see it when you first get it. Make sure that it is big enough for your parrot to fly through without hitting his wings and attach it to a stand that positions it at a height that will make it easy for him to fly through from his T-stand. To start training place it right in front of his training perch and set him on the perch, making sure he isn't afraid of it.

Step him up through the hoop, saying "good" as he steps through it and onto your hand. Then reward him. Next hop him through it using your recall. Then continue to use the recall to get him to flap his wings a couple of times to make the hop through. As you begin to get him to go farther to come through the hoop, reposition the hoop so that it is midway between you and your parrot. Stand on the other side of the hoop, directly across from him so that it is a straight shot and easiest to simply fly through to get to you.

Approximate slowly until you are ten feet or so away from the perch. Remember to mark the event the moment your parrot flies through the hoop. If at any time he

When your parrot is comfortable hopping through the hoop, back up a bit so he has to fly through to reach your hand.

Precisely mark the moment your parrot goes through the hoop so he understands what to do to earn the reward.

flies around the hoop, do not mark the event and do not reward him. Put him back onto the perch and come a little closer so that he is more likely to fly through the hoop. Say "good" when he does and reward him. Until he has a few experiences of missing the hoop and not having the event marked or rewarded, he probably is not going to understand the criteria.

Once you are calling him at about ten feet away, start moving slightly to the side of the hoop and calling him. Do small approximations so that he has to make a little bit more of an effort each time in order to include the hoop in his flight before he comes to you. If he misses, do not mark the event or give a reward; put him back onto the perch. Then go back to the last position you were in at which he was successful and call him again. Keep approximating farther to the side of the hoop until your parrot is making a wide arc to fly through the hoop and get to you. Next do all the same approximations on the other side of the hoop. Soon you have a parrot that will fly through the hoop whenever the hoop is out in the open and you do a recall.

Put Away Your Trash

Props Needed: Crumpled up paper, trash can
Cue: Presentation of paper, trash can and cue of "Clean it up"
Desired Behavior: Parrot flies to crumpled paper, picks up paper, puts it into trash can and repeats until all the paper is gone.
Steps:

1. Parrot (who already knows how to retrieve) placed on table next to crumpled paper looks at paper.
2. Follows target hand to paper next to him.
3. Picks up paper near edge of table.
4. Brings paper to the edge of table and drops it into trash can.
5. Takes paper from middle of table to drop it into trash can.
6. Takes paper from other side of table to drop it into trash can.
7. Takes paper from floor next to the table, follows target hand to fly up to table to drop it into trash can.
8. Takes paper from farther away to fly over and drop into trash can.
9. Takes multiple pieces of paper to trash can.

Instructions

If your parrot has already learned a retrieve this should be a fairly quick train, especially if he has multiple behaviors that involve a retrieve on cue. You will find that he quickly generalizes that what he is picking up this time is a crumpled piece of paper and that the receptacle is a trash can.

Start by placing a crumpled piece of paper near the edge of your table. Put an open trash can underneath it, and then place your parrot onto the table.

Using your target hand, direct your parrot to the paper. When he touches it say "good." If he drops it when you say "good," you can still reward him. If he's a retrieval pro, he may immediately start looking for where you want him to put it. Lead him with your target hand to the edge of the table and hold the trash can directly underneath him at the table edge. When he drops it in, mark the event and reward him. Set him up to succeed in the next few approximations by holding the trash can in an easy place for him to drop the paper and make her it in.

Then place the trashcan on the floor so that he has to walk over to it and drop the paper from directly above in order to get it in. In your next approximations, move the paper farther away from the edge of the table. Use your target hand to lead your parrot to the paper if necessary and then use your target hand to direct him to the dropping-off spot. Once your parrot is picking up the paper wherever you put it on the table and dropping it into the trash can with minimal guidance from your target hand, you can start working in the flying aspect of the trick.

Place a piece of paper on the floor near the table, being careful to place it so that your parrot has an easy angle for flying up to the table. Then set your parrot down next to the paper. When he picks it up, target him to the table where he

You can easily add flight to the basic retrieve, as shown here with a crow.

An outdoor aviary allows your parrot to experience some outdoor flight while eliminating many of the dangers of the outside world.

can drop the paper into the trash can. Flying with the paper in his beak may be a challenge. If it is, you can take some time to approximate flying with the paper by giving him the paper and then having him step, hop, and then fly to your perch hand, marking the event and rewarding him only if he keeps the paper in his beak until he lands on your hand.

Once he is picking up the paper and flying it to the table to drop it into the trash can, you can put multiple pieces of paper on the floor. When he drops the first piece of paper, target him to the next. Lead him through the steps only when he seems stuck. Soon you will have a parrot that will gather up papers and deposit them into the trash one by one. This behavior is a crowd pleaser, and it gives your parrot a way to get exercise and keep out of trouble at the same time.

Going Further with Flying Behaviors

Those are just a couple of behaviors that you could train with a flighted parrot. Using some of the tricks and behaviors your parrot has learned in the earlier chapters, you can come up with your own fun games for your parrot to enjoy. With a parrot that is flighted, giving him games he can play and tasks he can complete on the wing will make managing him much easier. Remember that one of the most valuable tools to combat unwanted behavior is to train an incompatible behavior. A parrot cannot be gathering paper and chewing on the baseboards at the same time. There is a tremendous amount of value in this training!

Outdoor Flying

If you enjoy the idea of having a free-flighted parrot and have success with training yours, you may begin to think about flying your parrot outside. Think this through very carefully. Even if you have tremendous confidence in your parrot's recall and flight skills, there are many things that can go awry with your parrot if he is flying and exploring outside.

There are more possibilities for danger to a free-flying parrot outdoors than you likely realize. You have probably already considered predators. Hawks, falcons, dogs, cats, coyotes, and many other dangerous predators abound outside. While parrots do have some instincts for avoiding predators, there is a lot to learn about avoiding and evading other dangerous animals. In a flock, a parrot would learn this from his peers. He would also learn what he should and should not

Bigger Isn't Better

Sometimes when you are training, your parrot just does not seem to get it. Inevitably when the parrot stares at us blank-eyed and without moving a feather, we start cuing bigger. We get louder and make the physical cue larger. Pretty soon we are practically yelling and waving our arms. Bigger is not better when you are trying to get a parrot to respond to a cue. It is not any more likely to get a response. If your parrot does not offer the behavior you are asking for, stop cuing and turn you back for moment. Then try again.

eat. A free-flying parrot may taste poisonous berries or even drink tainted water outside. He could also fly into traffic, fly into a window, or land on wires connected to a transformer and be electrocuted. It might be healthier for him to have an opportunity to fly like a wild bird, but it is also very possible he could be killed.

That said, I fly a peregrine. I adore every hunting season, and he faces all of the same dangers, perhaps even more. My peregrine hunts, which automatically creates even riskier situations. I believe that he is a wild animal and in order for me to do what is right by him, he needs to be allowed to fly and hunt outside. I feel this is true even though he was bred in captivity. Every season I prepare myself for a hard goodbye, knowing that my time with him is likely borrowed.

I do think my parrots might have a better quality of life if I used my skills to train them to fly outside as well. In fact, I've helped train more than a hundred birds, including many parrots, to free-fly outside. However, I am not willing to risk my parrots' deaths. This is an emotional and personal decision

You will need to invest many hours of training time before your parrot can be allowed to fly free outdoors.

The Perfectly Trained Parrot

for which I take complete responsibility. I urge you to think through completely the big picture of flying your parrot outside as I have and make an informed decision.

If you decide to fly your parrot outside, I also urge you to seek informational resources. I could write another entire book on the nuances and possibilities for training birds to fly outside. You will find that there is a tremendous amount to learn, and the repercussions of not learning could be immense. There are online groups, blogs, and workshops for outdoor free-flight that you can participate in. If you live in a major metropolitan area, you may even be able to find some people who are working on training their birds for outdoor flight. It is much better to have peers than to try to learn to train your parrot in a vacuum. Every individual bird is a different training challenge with different quirks, preferences, and talents. You can learn a lot from watching other people training their parrots and sharing information. And above all else, invest in hours, months, and years of time training your parrot.

Using a Harness

A better solution to taking your parrot outside can be using a harness. If your parrot is comfortable wearing a harness, you can take him outside and have more control over the potential dangers he can encounter. You still have to be vigilant about potential predators and obstacles, but at least you can keep your parrot closer so you can assist if there is trouble. Just keep in mind that there is training involved even in wearing a harness.

Follow the instructions in Chapter Five for teaching your parrot to allow you to put on the harness. Then you need to do some work to make sure your parrot understands the limitations and possibilities of wearing his harness. Work on recall indoors with your parrot. Go through all the same steps you have without the harness, only this time while he is wearing it. You want your parrot to have a positive history with wearing it before you take him outside.

You may think that just getting to go outside is a positive experience for your parrot, but if he has not spent time outdoors and in new places it may be terrifying. Your parrot will see things he has never seen before and may be startled by unexpected occurrences that are beyond your control. You do not want to take him outside wearing a harness if he has had no experience wearing it. What if a car

Take the time to train your parrot to wear a harness outside. If you rush him into this, he may become frightened of the harness.

backfires and startles him? He may try to fly in an effort to escape the frightening noise only to get yanked at the end of the harness lead, startling him further and maybe even causing him discomfort. If this is how he experiences wearing a harness, he isn't going to want to wear it and go outside.

Give him a chance to learn the limitations of his harness. And try to set him up to have positive experiences outside. Pay attention to his body language and note things that are making him nervous. Then take the time to desensitize him and allow him to experience new things in a way that is enjoyable. Remember to always

Food Management

If you are working with an adult parrot that has very little experience with flying, you may find that you need more motivation from your bird than you have with training any other trick. Fortunately, you do not need to deprive your parrot to get him more interested in food. All you need to do is pay attention to how much your parrot actually eats each day. Then rather than leaving him with food in his bowl all day long, ration this same amount out in two or three meals. Save his favorite food for training, but give him a portion of his normal rations after the session. Let him eat until he is done and then remove his food bowl. You will find that he is more interested in treats.

have the end of the harness lead attached to you. You never want your parrot to fly off harness lead and all. He could get tangled where you cannot reach him and be injured or killed.

Conclusion

Having a flighted parrot is a controversial topic. There are many strong opinions about this, but the most important one is yours. Be responsible and think your position through, but in the end it is you who has to live with your decisions and your parrot. I do not always agree with the choices that people make regarding living with their parrots. Then again, I don't always agree with the way humans treat each other when they share space either. To me a relationship that works trumps all my opinions. I believe it is more essential that the connection and interactions between a parrot and his person are so enjoyable that the thought of giving up your parrot would never cross your mind.

Learning to Fly (Again)

Ty has taken to going on walkabouts. In the "new" house with its open floor plan and circular paths we all seem to get the urge to wander. The thing is, though, if I had wings I wouldn't climb from my perch and waddle to my destination.

I let Ty learn to fly before he learned to do without. I brought him home when he was six weeks old, barely sprouting a red tail. I watched him feather up, slim down, and take to the air. It happened in no time at all, from penguin waddle to finessing the air. Ty was a competent, even nimble flier before I clipped his wings.

Clipping a bird's wings is a personal decision and often a good one to make. When Ty was clipped, however, he took spills, hard ones that flayed the thin skin on his breastbone and bruised the wrists of his wings. And as soon as I discovered what a disaster he was without a full-length of primary feathers, I let him grow them back out. And when his feathers grew back out, he flew again, but I was super cautious. I discouraged flying and arranged play areas so that there was no place to fly to. Over the years Ty just stopped flying altogether.

I'm sure it's "just like riding a bicycle; you never forget."—which, by the way, is a ridiculous metaphor if you're clumsy. Have you ever climbed onto a bicycle after a fifteen-year hiatus? It's terrifying. Sure, you will remember how to balance, brake, and turn, but what you immediately remember is what it felt like to fall. You remember skinned knees, road rash, and maybe even broken bones. Perhaps you even remember what it felt like when your friends laughed as you wiped out. You can never go back to not knowing how hard it was to learn to the first time. The possibility of the physical and emotional pain is huge.

So watching Ty waddle risk-free across the floor instead of flying has made me a little sad. It's odd, but he also makes me think about writing. I haven't touched my novel in three weeks. Halfway through the manuscript and I've been thinking that maybe I should just set the book-writing aside for a while. There seems to be so little point to writing books anyway. What is the harm in stopping for a while, maybe a long while? You can always come back to it later.

Then the other day Ty flew from his cage to the couch where he could look out the window. He looked both exhilarated and terrified. Flying in a confined space is like writing and so many other things worth doing. It will never be easy. There is just too much to navigate.

Maybe learning to fly again is even harder.

So don't quit a passion, even if it's hard and scary. And if you're starting again, good for you! Now keep going. Nothing really worth doing is easy, but you get better at it.

With some coaching, I'm sure I can get Ty flying again, and maybe his efforts will remind me to stay on the wing as well. If you too want your parrot to fly, be patient and understanding. Learning to fly is harder than it looks!

9

What's Next?

hope that as you work through the chapters and find more and more success with your parrot you will discover that training is fun and not that hard for you. If you find that certain aspects of this book do not make sense to you, there are a lot of great resources out there that you can tap into. Many of them are even free. Look for resources that depend on applied behavior analysis for answers to behavior problems and depend on operant conditioning with positive reinforcement for training. If it turns out that you have a knack for training and want to just get out there and do something with your new-found talents, there are also many ways to use your skills that are helpful and fun.

There are numerous online resources for parrot training, including how-to videos, forums, and workshops.

Taking Classes & Going to Workshops
Online Learning

There are many additional resources that you can investigate online. There are Yahoo groups and discussion boards that discuss training and problem-solving behavior. Even if you do not enjoy joining in on these sorts of discussions, you can still learn a lot by lurking. There is a clicker training Yahoo chat group called Bird Click that may interest you. And if you search under pet birds, you will find free-flight groups and even groups that are specific to different species of parrots. While you will get varying levels of information, this is a nice place to look for like minds and the best places to learn.

There are a few workshops you can also attend online. If your main interest is managing problem behaviors, I highly recommend Dr. Susan Friedman's class, *Living and Learning with Parrots for Caregivers*. This eight-week course run through a closed email list will teach you how to use the concepts of applied behavior analysis. You can also find a Yahoo group for Parrot Behavior Analysis Solutions (PBAS) that is an excellent continuation of developing your skills after you have taken the course. You can find all the information for this on Dr. Friedman's Behavior Works website (behaviorworks.org).

If you just need a little encouragement or need some visuals to see what a

Sifting Through Online Resources

Not all online resources are good ones, and when you are new to training it can be hard to tell what you should be ignoring and what you should be paying attention to online. I am frequently disheartened by videos with a million views that are misinterpreted or flat out wrong. Just because everyone is watching it or reading it does not make it good information. It just makes it viral. If you have ever spent time on Snopes.com, then you've seen how much that is viral is actually true—almost none of it! Good information will be linked by reputable resources. Check the blogs and expert sites you follow for links and discussions. And the wonderful thing about the Internet is that you can also ask sources you trust if you are not sure about the validity of the information you have found elsewhere.

behavior should look like, you can also search on YouTube for videos of trained parrots. Sometimes it helps to see how the final result looks. You will also find some great short instructional clips on Barbara Heidenreich's Good Bird, Inc. YouTube page and her website (goodbirdinc.com). If you feel that visual examples of training would be especially helpful, but do not want to leave your home, I recommend purchasing Good Bird, Inc.'s parrot training videos. All are excellent and use operant conditioning with positive reinforcement.

Classroom Learning

There are many opportunities to take classes and hear professionals speak on positive reinforcement and training parrots with operant conditioning. If you live in a major metropolitan area you should be able to find some classes to attend. Start by looking at local bird clubs. Many bird clubs have monthly meetings and invite relevant speakers to talk on training and parrot care. I have frequently spoken at bird clubs and find that the bird club members are enthusiastic and enjoyable

There are many opportunities to take classes and hear professionals speak on positive methods for training parrots.

A Word About Experts

The Internet has given rise to hordes of people who refer to themselves as experts. For the most part, no one checks credentials. Anyone can put together a slick website, fabricate their experience, supply endorsements from people who do not exist, and then sell a sloppy e-book, claiming to be an expert. The problem is that their information may be outdated or even completely wrong. Worse, you may have shelled out your hard-earned money for a scam. Do a little bit of digging when you find "experts" on the Internet trying to sell you something. Check to see that these people are making appearances, have strong training resumes, publish materials traditionally as well as online, and that real people are saying positive things about them.

people with whom to spend an evening. After all, we have a lot in common! Members often bring birds, and I hear them swapping stories about their parrots and sharing information. Bird clubs in general are fantastic resources.

Another place to look for further opportunities to learn is with local parrot advocacy organizations. Many non-profit organizations that re-home parrots also offer classes for free or for a very reasonable charge. Groups such as Phoenix Landing in Virginia and Parrot Education and Adoption Center (PEAC), which has locations in San Diego, Cleveland, Pittsburgh, and Anchorage, offer fantastic educational opportunities. In fact, many advocate organizations require that anyone adopting a parrot complete training for parrot care. These organizations and others sometimes offer classes and workshops taught by experienced trainers. Keep an eye out for day-long workshops that allow you to bring your parrot and allow you to do some hands-on training with instruction and with your own parrot. It can be particularly helpful to have a practiced bird trainer talking you through the training.

There are also retreats and weekend or even week-long workshops that you can attend. Those are more expensive options, but if you want to work one-on-one with professional trainers and hands-on with parrots you can consider them.

Watch for opportunities for events like this on BirdChannel.com and elsewhere online. In the last couple of years there has even been a Parrot Lover's Cruise that offered seminars. Just be sure to do a little research on whoever is speaking to make sure that they have good credentials!

Helping Others

In the animal-training world it is very common for individuals to have some success training a few animals and then decide that they know it all. Heck, I thought I knew it all 20 years ago, but I still learn something new every time I train a new animal. The problem is that we jump to conclusions about why the things we do work without having enough information to truly understand why the animal responded the way it did. We also assume that we can teach others to train their parrots exactly the way we trained ours. However, the challenges involved with training every behavior will change with every animal, because all animals are individuals with a personality and a range of experiences unique to them. Even if you have worked with hundreds of birds and a variety of species, you should be very careful about presenting yourself as an expert.

Leading by Example

If you have success training your parrot some tricks, of course you should share video and stories online! You should, that is, if you are comfortable with doing so.

If you have the time and space, fostering a parrot is a wonderful way to help a parrot adoption agency.

In fact, I would love to see your videos. There is nothing that makes me happier than to see a parrot owner having a blast with his or her parrot. I also just love to waste time watching parrots doing things online that make me smile and laugh. You should be proud of yourself and your parrot for your successes! Just remember that there is a big difference between being a successful trainer and a successful teacher of trainers. Additionally, being polite, kind, and helpful to others online will do more good for parrots than condemning people will.

Leading by example and sharing information is something much needed in the parrot community. The Internet could use more blogs and videos of parrot training done right! Antiquated ideas still linger in the common beliefs of bird owners. Many people still think that parrots are "just birds" and that training them is impossible. These people believe that parrots are just meant to be pretty and sit in a cage. Others think that the way you manage a parrot is to show him who's boss and that parrots will dominate you if you let them. People like this need to see more parrot owners interacting positively and having a good time with their birds. These misinformed parrot owners could discover through you that parrots can be very well behaved. Sharing your successes and the resources that helped you become successful can make the world a better place for others!

Volunteering

You can put your new training skills to use and help other parrots by volunteering. There are hundreds of organizations working to re-home parrots that have been relinquished. Some of these places house parrots in facilities where you can volunteer your time to feed, care for, and interact with the parrots. These parrots still need socialization. And sometimes these facilities need people to work with them to make sure they get play time out of their cage. It is also helpful to see what their temperaments are like and whether or not they interact positively with people. If a parrot is hand shy, it is nice to have someone work with getting the parrot to step up on cue. Check around and see whether there is anywhere you can volunteer a bit of your time.

If you have more time to invest and space in your home, fostering a parrot is even better. The majority of parrot welfare organizations do not have very much space to house transitioning parrots and instead depend on the homes of

Keep it Short

If you put together your own routine with your parrot or a couple of your parrots, keep it to 20 minutes or less with multiple birds. Less is better if you just have one bird. I did shows for years and can guarantee that people's attention span does not last any longer than 20 minutes for funny parrot tricks. Any longer than that and eyes begin to glaze over and people start getting irritated with you for not wrapping things up. Also your parrot may not be likely to hang in there for a routine longer than ten minutes. If shows are long and taxing on your parrot, he is likely to quit on you.

volunteers to foster birds. These birds stay temporarily until they are adopted. This can be a few weeks or months depending on the bird and the demand for the species. If you can keep a space in your home and discipline yourself to not keep every parrot you foster, you can do a lot of good.

When you foster a parrot, if you take the time to teach it some behaviors you help the bird become more socialized and comfortable with people. You can also assist in helping the parrot learn more desirable behaviors and things that can help him for the rest of his life. Who wouldn't be happy to discover that the parrot they are adopting has been trained to step up, go into a carrier, and allow you to trim his toenails? You can help set this parrot up to succeed in his new home. And if you train him to do a few tricks, he will also be more charming. You don't want someone to adopt a parrot just because he does tricks, but with so many

When your parrot does something cute or fun, like hanging upside down, try to get it on cue so you can make it part of your routine.

parrots available for adoption, it doesn't hurt to give your foster parrot a wing up! If you can convince someone who was thinking of buying a parrot to adopt your charming foster parrot, you have done an even bigger good deed.

Another thing that you can do to make a difference is to put your show on the road. If you have a parrot that is comfortable traveling and being in new places,

Avian Diseases

If you take your parrot out into places where there are other birds, you should definitely think about the possibility of avian diseases. There are diseases like psittacine beak and feather disease (PBFD) and proventricular dilatation disease (PDD), which are currently not easy to contain and have no cure. Talk to your avian veterinarian and see what he or she thinks about the possibilities of transmissible diseases. You will have to decide for yourself whether you feel there is much risk and whether or not you want to take the risk, but your vet can help you be more fully informed.

you might want to think about bringing a little bit of light into other people's lives. There is not a lot of money in the business of training parrots, but there sure are a lot of smiles. When you bring a trained parrot to a second grade class and talk about positive training, being kind to one another, and how amazing parrots are in the wild you may have given a child an experience that could change his or her life. It might even some day change the world for parrots.

There are also places that truly appreciate the beauty and smiles that a parrot brings into the room. A little parrot show at the local senior center or a nursing home can really brighten someone's day. It is great practice for your parrot and a wonderful way to volunteer your time. In fact, if you do a show at a nursing home, be sure to post it on YouTube! I would love to see it.

Putting Together Your Own Show

There are so many different things you can do to put together a parrot routine. Some of the funniest routines I have seen involve very simple behaviors interspersed with amusing dialogue. They did not really require the parrot to be able to do anything complicated at all. For example, Sunni Black did this wonderful routine with an Amazon parrot named Lolita in the late 1980s. There are a few videos of it on the Internet; the best is her appearance on Johnny Carson's show. The meat of Lolita's routine was this absolutely horrible song she sang. It was one verse of nonsense words, "la da di dah" and it was far from melodic. Sunni would build it up like she was going to sing something wonderful and ask her to do it for the audience. Lolita would sing this same line a few times and the audience would laugh. Then Sunni would say, "Okay, next verse," and Lolita would sing a few more lines of the same, eliciting more laughter from the audience. Sunni would suggest to the audience, "You can sing along" and they would laugh some more. Lastly she would ask Lolita for her "big finish," which would be, you guessed it, the same nonsense unmelodic line one last time. It was Sunni's delivery of her lines that made Lolita's routine so funny. So you do not need anything spectacular to put together a routine. You just need a good imagination and an excellent delivery.

When you start to think about what you want to put into a routine, play to your parrot's strengths. Some parrots are great talkers, some have larger than life body language, and some are great at tricks and obstacle courses. Think about what your parrot does at home

You never know what will happen with kids and animals. Brush up on your improv skills.

Improv—A Life Skill!

They say in show business that you should never work with animals and children. This thought has run through my mind many a time when things went awry on stage. Chances are that if you take your parrots out to do performances you will have moments when things fall apart for you as well. In fact, assume it will happen every time and brush up on your improvisation skills. Memorize a couple of parrot jokes to fill time when your bird decides he doesn't want to put the ball into the basket. Pay attention to the laughs you get by accident and get them on purpose next time. Most of all, learn to go with the flow and have fun. If you can think on your feet with a parrot running amok in a classroom of children, just imagine how well you will do at your next cocktail party or business negotiation!

that makes you laugh and capture some of those behaviors and get them on cue. If your parrot makes a sound that gets everyone's attention, perhaps the sound of a trash truck backing up—get it on cue.

Talking Routine

If your parrot is a talker, you can do a five-minute routine with a variety of noises and words that show off your parrot's abilities. Some species of parrots tend to talk more clearly, like African greys and Amazons. Some species seem to pick up singing with gusto, like Amazons. If your parrot sings or talks, think about the things you can teach him to say. Or you can start listening to the things he already says and think about how you might work that into a routine if you got it on cue. I love talking routines because with a little thought you can do a routine that isn't like anyone else's. Here's an example of a short script I might use with things my African grey parrot already says. The cues are in bold (R is me and T is Ty):

R: This is Ty. He's an African grey <u>parrot</u>.

T: I'm a chicken hawk.

R: No. You're a <u>parrot</u>.

T: I'm a chicken hawk.

R: Fine. You're a <u>hawk</u>.

T: And you're a chicken. Bok bok bok.

R: You're quite the comedian. Isn't he <u>funny</u>?

T: Ha ha ha ha.

R: So Ty, I was just telling everyone how smart you are. Can you demonstrate your math skills? How about 12 divided by **3**?

T: Four.

R: The square root of 49 minus **3**?

T: Four

R: You all had to think about that, didn't you? See, he's smart. He's no drip!

T: Plunk! Plunk! (Water dripping sound)

R: Wow. How did you make that sound without lips? Okay, **back up**.

T: Beep. Beep. Beep. (Truck backing up sound)

R: Very **funny**.

T: Ha ha ha!

R: Ty! **Guess what**?

T: Parrot butt.

R: Again. Very **funny**.

T: Ha ha ha.

R: Enough already. I'm trying to say it's time to go. Can you say **goodbye**?

T: Goodbye!

R: And that was Ty, the African grey parrot.

That whole routine had only eight cues and you could even cut it in half and it would still be entertaining. You

Training your parrot to run a small obstacle course is sure to be entertaining!

just have to make sure when you train that you choose cues that are versatile and work in context with the sound. For example, "back up" as a cue for the sound of a truck backing up could be used in a lot of different ways in a routine. So play around with scripts. Once you start working on training a script, be patient. As you train, start with asking the first line and then add the others one by one. You should add another line with a cue in it only when your parrot has done the others correctly. With some practice your parrot is likely to learn them all in order and respond quickly.

Body Language Routine

Some of the funniest routines I've seen with a parrot involve almost no sound at all. If you have a parrot with big body language you can have a blast building a routine for the bird. Cockatoos seem to be especially adept at this with their raised crests and tendency to dance.

R: This is Dalek. She's a sulfur-crested cockatoo. Can you **say hi**?

Dalek waves.

R: Be polite. They **can't hear you**.

D: Helllooooo!

R: She's pretty enthusiastic. This parrot loves to **party**.

Dalek dances.

R: Dalek, this isn't a dance party. **Get serious**.

D: Whooooo!

R: Okay, Dalek obviously needs to get this out of her system. Maybe we should have a dance contest. I need a volunteer. (Choose a little kid that's 5-8 years old from the audience.) Okay, stay where you are and I'm going to have each of you do a little routine and we'll see who wins. You know how to dance, right? Just pretend you're at a **party**.

Dalek dances.

R: Dalek, wait your **turn**.

Dalek turns in a circle.

R: Ha ha. Very funny. Okay, first up is our volunteer. Show us your best routine. (Kid dances.) Yay! That was awesome. Now, Dalek, it's your **turn**.

Dalek turns in a circle.

R: No, Dalek. I meant dance. You're the one who wanted to **party**.

Dalek dances.

R: Nice. What do you think, everyone? I think that was a tie. (Audience claps.) Great job, both of you. Thanks for coming out here, Dalek. Can you tell everyone **"goodbye"**?

D: Goodbye!

R: That was Dalek, the sulfur-crested cockatoo!

That was a fun routine with only six learned behaviors and an easy one for most cockatoos. To train a cockatoo to dance, all you have to do is dance with the bird and get her going and then capture the behavior. Other parrots may require a bit more shaping, but it is a simple behavior to train and very similar to "Training the Eagle," which is discussed in Chapter 6.

Obstacle Course Routine

To set up an obstacle course routine all you need to do is get out your props and string together the behaviors that you have taught your parrot. You can write a witty introduction if you wish, but more than anything else people will be impressed by your parrot's ability to complete a variety of tasks. A couple of clever sentences before each behavior will help move the routine along as well. Your routine might look something like this:

> This is Loki. She is a very talented Senegal parrot. In fact, she kind of runs the household, and my house is pretty crazy. Loki has it down, though. She watches over the finances and makes sure we save every **cent**. (Loki puts coins in piggy bank.) It's hard work managing our day-to-day activities, though. Loki says that sometimes it feels like an **obstacle course**. (Loki runs through tunnel, climbs up ladder, and slides down slide.) And it is hard work making sure everyone gets where they need to be. She says she feels like a **chauffeur** sometimes. (Loki pulls wagon with little toy figure in it.) And it's hard to keep all the balls in the air and get them where they need to be, like this **ball** for example. (Loki picks up ball and puts it into the basket.) At the end of the day, she's **dead** on her feet. (Loki plays dead.) But every day she gets back up and goes back at it because she's a real trooper, right, Loki? **Get up**. (Loki gets up and trainer picks her up.) Isn't she amazing? Thanks Loki! **Wave** goodbye. (Loki waves).

I hope this has given you a few ideas of ways you can incorporate your tricks into a routine that is entertaining. If you are doing a show outside your home, be sure to talk a bit about how you train, how much work you've put into creating your little superstar, and how parrots—while wonderful and fascinating creatures— aren't the right pets for everyone. Do tell everyone that it would be a tragedy to lose a single species in the wild and explain how many parrots are losing their natural habitats at a rapid rate. Take the opportunity to inspire people to care and wonder about the future for these fabulous and incredibly intelligent animals. Remember that your parrot is an ambassador for all the parrots that cannot show people how wonderful they are.

Ideas for Other Behaviors to Train

Here is a list of a few more ideas of things you can train to use in a routine.

- Whisper: Parrot leans in and mumbles or whispers to trainer.
- Roller Skate: Parrot rides bird-sized roller skate.
- Raise the Flag: Pulls a string to raise a flag up a tiny flagpole.
- Give Me a Kiss: Leans in and presents beak for a kiss.
- Nod Yes: Shakes head up and down.
- Nod No: Shakes head side to side.
- Shake Hands: Lifts one foot and shakes.
- Open a Soda Can: Pulls tap, popping the top on an aluminum can.
- Hang Upside Down: Drops upside-down on hand or perch.
- Sing a Song: Learn to sing and offer a verse of a song on cue.
- Dance: Bobs head and lifts wings repeatedly on cue.
- Bow: Parrot puts foot and wing out in a stretch and bows head.

Taking the Show on the Road

Just because your parrot is performing like a champ at home, don't assume that he will do his routine anywhere you take him. It is natural for a parrot to freeze up when he gets into an environment he has not seen before. If you want to take him places to perform, give him chances to do his tricks in front of an audience in your home. Then take him to your parents' house or a friend's place. Gradually introduce him to a variety of places, environments, and people so that he learns to be confident no matter where he is performing.

Move Me

I did the math: in his 17 years Ty has moved to a different residence more than a dozen times, one more than a dozen, in fact. The last move was lucky number 13.

We made the first move from a condo in Riverside when Ty was only two and had just started to label his world. This was after a stalker shattered a youthful belief in my immortality and forced me, with my head low, back to my father. Once I nursed my wounds and gathered my courage it was time to hit the road again. Our next move took four days of driving and taught me that Ty can be very demanding about bedtimes on the road. His "good nights" got so insistent that I pulled into a hotel early one night just to get him to shut up. So we landed in Florida to start over.

We lived on the ranch where I was training birds. We stayed in a trailer affectionately dubbed "The Velvet Elvis" until I found an apartment with a view of a lake and an eagle's nest. Ty learned to cackle like a bald eagle and mimic grackles. Then we relocated to Ohio for a summer, where I managed a brand-new bird show at the Toledo Zoo. Living in the office, Ty learned to mimic an old school fax machine and a phone ring so pitch perfect that he annoyed my boss, who came running every time. From there we went to the Texas State Fair in Dallas, Ty mumbling under my plane seat the whole way. And when I got sick and scared and lonely for family, we drove back to California so I could lick my wounds again. Ty said, "Bye! See you later!" when we crossed the California border and we barely made it past the perplexed border guard.

After that we spent six months house-sitting in the rural desert mountains, where Ty learned to call Stump the dog and wonder "Where ARE you" after the tortoises in my care. Then we landed in the La Quinta apartment where my falcon Anakin changed my world view and

Ty narrated my early mornings. Then I bought a house and there Ty learned to mimic the sound of fledging red-tailed hawks and howl like the neighborhood dogs against the fire truck sirens, and he laughed, a lot.

Two years ago we moved for a dream job. I still had the job, but hated the house so we moved again. I don't know if Ty hated it too or succumbed to my unhappiness, but it was a quiet year and half. It was the only place that even Ty couldn't make home. So I wisely moved us.

Ty is in fine form again in this house where he can survey the kitchen, living room and office from his cage. There's no escaping his commentary now. His newest phrase is my favorite: a plaintive, "You're killing me, dog." I didn't even realize that I said that to my Brittany, but I have to laugh.

Surely, this place will be temporary too, but I'm hoping for a few less transitory years. Not that Ty seems to mind. He has brought a bit of every place we've ever lived along for the ride. Ty seems to know that home sounds like the wild outside, the routines that don't change, and the laughter you bring with you. And I guess I don't mind either. I'll move 13 times more as long as Ty can come with me.

I hope that you find this sort of joy in your parrot as well. Whether he talks or sings or dances, I hope you find your own brand of fun and a lifetime of joy in training it.

Conclusion

started this book by telling you that training could change your life. If you find you love training birds, that you have a talented parrot, and that the both of you want to share the fun with others, it really will change your world. The two cockatiels I trained to do tricks when I was nine years old certainly led me on a path that shaped my life. (Although to this day I don't understand why no one came to the neighborhood pet talent show I put together. I had made flyers and had another judge and everything. Perhaps I was ahead of my time in fourth grade.) I hope that if you discover as much joy in training as I did you will find me at www.heckledbyparrots.com and share your successes. Maybe it's not too late for me to finally have that neighborhood pet talent show I wanted when I was a little kid. It will just have to be on the Web instead.

Even if you do not train dozens of tricks and create elaborate routines, I hope you discover that training your parrot to do a couple of things adds a new dimension to your relationship. I hope it helps you realize the possibilities and how easy it is to shape good behavior just by being mindful and clear in your communication. Perhaps it will even turn out that I was right about how it can shift the human relationships in your life to more positive connections as well. And if you use positive reinforcement to teach your boyfriend to put his socks into the laundry basket or your girlfriend to wait until after the game to talk to you, let me know that too. I won't tell.

If you learn a few things in this book that are useful to you, don't stop here. Find other resources and learn as much as you can. The possibilities for training are limitless. The science is available, and people are discovering clever and amazing uses for applied behavior analysis all the time. What is happening in the field of animal training is fascinating, and it's so exciting that it is creating a more positive world for the animals in our lives. I hope that it makes for a more positive world for you as well.

Resources

Clubs and Societies

American Federation of Aviculture, Inc.
PO Box 91717
Austin, TX 78709
Telephone: 512-585-9800
Fax: 512-858-7029
E-mail: afaoffice@afabirds.org
www.AFAbirds.org

Avicultural Society of America
E-mail: info@asabirds.org
www.asabirds.org

International Association of Avian Trainers
www.IAATE.org

Further Learning and Online Classes

Behavior Works
www.behaviorworks.org
Susan Friedman's site where individuals can sign up for online "Living and Learning with Parrots" classes.

GoodBird Inc
www.goodbirdinc.com
Barbara Heidenreich's site where individuals can find in-person workshops in their area.

Karen Pryor Academy
www.karenpryoracademy.com
Karen Pryors school offering online and in person classes on operant conditioning.

Natural Encounters
www.naturalencounters.com
Animal trainer, Steve Martin's site where individuals can find week-long bird training workshops in Florida.

Publications

Videos

Captive Foraging: The Next Best Thing to Being Free. Dr. M. Scott Echols

Parrot Behavior and Training. GoodBird, Inc.

Training Your Parrot for the Veterinary Exam. GoodBird, Inc.

Training Your Parrot to Talk. Good Bird, Inc

Magazines

Good Bird
PO Box 684394
Austin, TX 78768
www.GoodBirdInc.com

Parrots Magazine
The Old Cart House
Applesham Farm
Coombes
West Sussex BN15 0RP
United Kingdom
www.parrotmag.com

Books

Good Bird! A Guide to Solving Behavioral Problems in Companion Parrots. Barbara Heidenreich. Avian Publications

A Parrot for Life. Rebecca K. O'Connor. TFH Publications, Inc.

The Parrot Problem Solver. Barbara Heidenriech. TFH Publications, Inc.

Index

Note: **Boldfaced** numbers indicate illustrations.

Photo Credits

Rebecca K. O'Connor has trained birds professionally in zoos and private facilities around the United States and abroad. She has kept parrots personally for more than 30 years and is a nationally known parrot behaviorist. She is also a well-known falconer and has practiced falconry, the art of training birds of prey, for almost two decades. She is the author of the best-selling book, *A Parrot for Life: Raising and Training the Perfect Parrot Companion*, as well *Lories and Lorikeets* and *Finches*. She is also the author of the acclaimed falconry memoir *Lift*.

O'Connor is a nationally sought-after lecturer at parrot clubs and parrot festivals, speaking about training as well as the day-to-day experience of living with parrots. Her popular blog, Heckled by Parrots (www.heckledbyparrots.com), is a go-to resource for many parrot lovers, and she frequently speaks on radio shows.

In all of O'Connor's work she strives to illuminate the human condition through the animals that surround us. Whether it is to give a science-based lecture, write a serious how-to book, or to craft deeply personal prose, the foundation of everything in her life is a love for animals. She hopes that her life's work will help people understand the animals (including other humans) that surround them and relish their relationships. You can find her at www.rebeccakoconnor.com.